Women Authors of Detective Series

Also by Moira Davison Reynolds

*American Women Scientists:*
*23 Inspiring Biographies, 1900–2000*
(McFarland, 1999)

*Immigrant American Women Role Models:*
*Fifteen Inspiring Biographies, 1850–1950*
(McFarland, 1997)

*Women Advocates of Reproductive Rights:*
*Eleven Who Led the Struggle in*
*the United States and Britain*
(McFarland, 1994)

*Women Champions of Human Rights:*
*Eleven U.S. Leaders of the Twentieth Century*
(McFarland, 1991)

*Nine American Women of the Nineteenth Century:*
*Leaders into the Twentieth*
(McFarland, 1988)

*Uncle Tom's Cabin and Mid-Nineteenth*
*Century United States*
(McFarland, 1985)

# Women Authors of Detective Series

## *Twenty-One American and British Writers, 1900–2000*

*by*

Moira Davison Reynolds

McFarland & Company, Inc., Publishers
*Jefferson, North Carolina, and London*

**Library of Congress Cataloguing-in-Publication Data**

Reynolds, Moira Davison.
Women authors of detective series : twenty-one American and British writers, 1900–2000 / by Moira Davison Reynolds.
p. cm.
Includes bibliographical references and index.
ISBN 0-7864-0982-7 (softcover : 50# alkaline paper) ♾
1. Detective and mystery stories, American—History and criticism. 2. Women and literature—United States—History—20th century. 3. Women and literature—Great Britain—History—20th century. 4. Detective and mystery stories, English—History and criticism. 5. Detective and mystery stories, American—Bio-bibliography. 6. Detective and mystery stories, English—Bio-bibliography. 7. American fiction—Women authors—History and criticism. 8. English fiction—Women authors—History and criticism. 9. American fiction—Women authors—Bio-bibliography. 10. English fiction—Women authors—Bio-bibliography. 11. Series (Publications)—Bibliography. I. Title.
PS374.D4R49 2001
813'.0872099287'0904—dc21 2001030515

British Library cataloguing data are available



Manufactured in the United States of America

*McFarland & Company, Inc., Publishers*
*Box 611, Jefferson, North Carolina 28640*
*www.mcfarlandpub.com*

To Isabelle Anne Reynolds,
beloved grandchild

# Contents

# Preface and Acknowledgments

The selection of authors to be profiled in this book had few criteria—only that the women, British and American, had written detective stories in series during the 20th century. From the many writers who qualified, I chose with an eye to interest and variety, both in the lives of the authors and in the characters they created. The result was that some selected were established writers, while others are just beginning their careers; some are serious, others light-hearted; and so on. For some, I found plenty of biographical material; for others, it is rather scant.

This book is for ordinary readers, especially those who are only slightly familiar with crime novels but would like to read more. With those readers in mind, I have in most cases tried to present the flavor of an author's work without revealing too much about any plot. I have also, through the chief investigators, tried to show something of the progress in women's emancipation during the past century.

I wish to acknowledge the constant assistance of the staff of Peter White Public Library, despite the inconvenience they suffered of being located in temporary premises while the library building undergoes expansion. Again I salute Joanne Whitley of Superiorland Library Cooperative for locating materials that are difficult to find.

Thanks to Mary Frey for producing an image of Dora Turnbull.

For suggestions about authors I am indebted to Anne Spear, Joanne Whitley, Earl Hilton, and Miriam Hilton.

I also wish to thank Lisl Cade for materials on Carol Higgins Clark.

Moira Davison Reynolds • Marquette, Michigan

# Introduction

This book focuses on 20th century British and American women authors of detective series. In most cases, detective fiction here implies a rational solution of a puzzle originating in a crime; it does not include, for example, spy, adventure, or horror stories.

The detective genre enjoyed its greatest popularity between the years 1925 and 1945, but its history goes back to the 19th century—beginning with Edgar Allan Poe, considered the father of the modern detective story. He created C. Auguste Dupin, who appeared in three stories: "The Murders in the Rue Morgue" (1841), "The Mystery of Marie Roget" (1843), and "The Purloined Letter" (1845). Authorities believe that Poe, an American, had read and was influenced by *Mémoires de Vidocq* (1828).

The eponymous hero of that book, François Eugene Vidocq, had an overpowering weakness for women; he was a forger, thief, and highwayman; he had lived among criminals in Paris, learning their ways. He had served eight years' hard labor in the galleys. Apparently assuming that it takes a thief to catch a thief, in 1809 he offered himself as a spy to the Paris police. His former experiences proved valuable, and he eventually became known for his effective work in finding criminals.

In England, the first detective novels were written by Wilkie Collins: *The Woman in White* (1860) and *The Moonstone* (1868). Ten years after *The Moonstone*, Anna Katharine Green wrote *The Leavenworth Case*, an early American detective novel. It has been claimed in recent years that *The Dead Letter* (1867) by American writer Metta Victoria Fuller Victor was the first full-length detective novel in English. Victor's pen name was Seeley Regester.

Making his debut in 1887, Arthur Conan Doyle's detective, Sherlock

Holmes, was on his way to world fame by the 1890s. Almost as well known was Dr. Watson, Holmes' companion.

Students of women's history note that *The Female Detective* (1864), edited by Andrew Forrester, Jr., presented Mrs. Gladden, the first professional female detective. Almost half a century later, Baroness Orczy of Scarlet Pimpernel fame wrote about a sleuth named Lady Molly of Scotland Yard.

An American woman did much to promote the popularity of the detective novel. Mary Roberts Rinehart (1876–1958) offered mysteries "to the reader who wants a novel, not merely a 'whodunit.'" Her books were best sellers continuously from 1909 to 1936. Poet Ogden Nash labeled her style "Had I But Known," and the label stuck. He was referring to cases exemplified by the young woman who wanders into a danger that she had been specifically warned to avoid.

Although people liked short stories about crime, detective novels, especially in series, were published in increasing numbers. Male writers used the genre—for example, Dashiell Hammett (with the character of Sam Spade); William Huntington Wright, writing as S.S. Van Dine (Philo Vance); Erle Stanley Gardner (Perry Mason); and Rex Stout (Nero Wolf).

Women have proved to be very successful mystery writers. The subjects of this book represent only a small proportion.

Somerset Maugham, the British novelist, predicted that "detection writing" would be studied in colleges and universities throughout the world and that "aspirants for doctoral degrees will shuttle the ocean and haunt the world's great libraries to conduct personal research expeditions into the lives and sources of the masters of the art." Time has proved Maugham correct. By 1977, 12 years after Maugham's death, academic and mystery writer Robert Parker stated that he had witnessed the dignification of the hard-boiled detective story. He referred to tenure-seeking professors of English who examine detective works in a frame—Freudian criticism, Marxist criticism, and so on. By such means, the study becomes a scholarly pursuit. The credentials of several of the subjects in this book show that detective novels have become legitimate objects of literary criticism and analysis, and that scholarly women are writing them.

The Hardy Boys and the Nancy Drew books introduced some readers to mystery fiction in their childhoods. These and other series were the creation of Edward Stratemeyer (1862–1930). He conceived story ideas, outlined plots and then hired writers to complete the works, which he sold to publishers, holding the rights himself. With this arrangement, several authors, all writing as Franklin W. Dixon, wrote Hardy Boys books. It is now known that Carolyn Keene is the pseudonym for more than one person. The original Nancy Drew books, introduced in the 1930s, were written by Mildred Wirt Benson. Benson was the first woman to earn a master's degree in journalism from the University of Iowa. After Stratemeyer's death in 1930, his daughter, Harriet Lane, had an important role in shaping Nancy Drew books. The Stratemeyer Syndicate was sold to Simon and Schuster in 1984. Up-to-date Nancy Drew mysteries are still in print and popular with young readers.

The popularity of the detective genre is undebatable. Howard Haycraft, critic and authority of the history of mysteries, wrote this about detective stories in 20th century life: "Perhaps the most striking illustration of the place the 'whodunit' has come to occupy in modern life occurred in London during the great blitz of 1940. Nightly, at the entrances to the fetid underground shelters, portable 'raid libraries' were set up to supply—by popular demand—mystery stories and nothing else." Writing in 1995, Klein stated that mystery fiction accounted for more than 20 percent of all books sold in the United States.

Readers of detective novels include eminent persons such as President Woodrow Wilson, Prime Minister Stanley Baldwin, General George Marshall, President Franklin Roosevelt, theologian Karl Bart, and Nobel laureate Henry Kissinger. President Lincoln read and reread Poe's tales.

There are varied opinions on why people read detective stories, and a satisfactory answer is not likely to be forthcoming. They obviously offer for some the vicarious pleasure of being clever. Mary Roberts Rinehart expressed another reason: "Our criminal instincts can only find a vicarious outlet in fiction." Bertrand Russell, the British philosopher and social reformer, said this: "Anyone who hopes that in time it may be possible to abolish war should give serious thought to the problem of satisfying harmlessly the instincts that we inherit from long generations of savages. For my part, I find a sufficient outlet in detective stories, where I alternately identify myself with the murderer and huntsman detective." Gladys Mitchell (see Chapter 6) did not believe that it was usual for people to read detective stories in order to learn new methods of committing murder, but she cited a case where a real-life murderer successfully employed a method described in a best-selling book. Some people look for escape. It is generally agreed that author Edmund Crispin spoke for many when he said, "The first and foremost aim [of detective stories] is to entertain." Detective story writer Jessica Mann holds the belief that crime novels reflect, rather than try to alter, the society in which and for which they are written. She contended that murder, among other passions, has always been of absorbing interest to those whose own lives lack it.

As the 20th century progressed, the settings of the stories changed drastically. The criminals and the investigators of later dates may seem to have little resemblance to their earlier counterparts, but essentially there is little difference. Robert Paul, author of *Whatever Happened to Sherlock Holmes,* made this observation: "Motive has always been recognized: money, social stigma, the temptation to eliminate some of life's more detested restraints—behind these there are people and the drives that come from personality—greed, pride and lust. 'Clues of character' provide important evidence for crime." We soon realize that the woman who kills her employer with a hatchet all for the love of a tea shop (*Funerals Are Fatal*, 1953) is not much different from the male murderer involved in a drug ring (*Dead Stick,* 1998).

Dorothy L. Sayers pointed out that the detective story proper could not flourish until public sympathy turned around to the side of law and order. As Great Britain's home secretary, Robert Peel brought about reform of the criminal laws and in 1829 established London's Metropolitan Police. He did so despite the opposition of his own Tory party, whose members regarded the police as a threat to personal liberty. Public acceptance of the unarmed police came slowly, but as crime diminished and law and order ruled, that acceptance increased. Dickens admired the police force; his *Bleak House* (1853) was the first novel in which the policeman was treated both realistically and sympathetically. By about 1860, police were known as Bobbies in honor of Robert Peel.

The headquarters of the Criminal Investigation Division (C.I.D.) was Scotland Yard, named after a narrow lane on which the rear entrance was located. The C.I.D. moved in 1890, gaining the name New Scotland Yard. Another move took place in 1967 to the Westminster area. New Scotland Yard is not the headquarters of the British police; there are independent complete police units throughout the United Kingdom. In particularly difficult cases, those units may seek advice from Scotland Yard.

Women have been officially employed by the C.I.D. since 1915. Since 1975, they have had equal rights with male officers.

In the United States, the establishment of New York City's police department in 1844 provided impetus for other cities to follow. The constable of colonial America survived in the rural sheriff.

Established in 1923, Interpol (International Criminal Police Organization) had headquarters in Vienna. With Hitler's invasion of Austria, it ceased to function effectively. Reestablished in 1946, it provides more than 140 member nations (which include the United States) with information regarding international criminals. Interpol has had its greatest success with regard to counterfeiting, forgery, smuggling, and the narcotics trade.

The Detection Club of London, founded in 1927, and the Crime Writers Association (C.W.A.), founded in 1953, are well known British organizations. The Detection Club insisted that its members put fairly before the reader every clue to the identity of the criminal. The C.W.A. set up awards, the Gold Dagger and the Silver Dagger, for the best English and best foreign mysteries of the year. In the United States, the Mystery Writers of America (M.W.A.), founded in 1945, presents worthy authors with "Edgars" and "Ravens" (in honor of Poe). In 1986, author Sara Paretsky was instrumental in founding Sisters in Crime to lobby for more book reviews of women authors and greater critical consideration.

Today, there are many mystery buffs who both glean from and contribute much information to the Internet. Awards given by fans include the Agatha (Malice Domestic mystery convention, devoted to traditional mystery), the Anthony (Bouchercon, the World Mystery Convention) and the Macavity (readership of the *Mystery Readers Journal* of Mystery Readers International).

The writers dealt with in this book are listed below, with nationality and year of birth (and death, if applicable). Well known pseudonyms are in parentheses.

| | | |
|---|---|---|
| Dora Turnbull (*Patricia Wentworth*) | British | 1879–1961 |
| Agatha Christie | British | 1890–1976 |
| Dorothy Sayers | British | 1893–1957 |
| Elizabeth Mackintosh (*Josephine Tey*) | British | 1897–1952 |
| Ngaio Marsh | New Zealand | 1899–1982 |
| Gladys Mitchell | British | 1901–1983 |
| Margery Allingham | British | 1904–1966 |
| Edith Pargeter (*Ellis Peters*) | British | 1913–1995 |
| Phyllis Dorothy James White (*P.D. James*) | British | 1920– |
| Gwendoline Butler (*Jennie Melville*) | British | 1920– |
| Patricia Highsmith | American | 1921–1995 |
| Carolyn Heilbrun (*Amanda Cross*) | American | 1926– |
| Ruth Rendell | British | 1930– |
| Edna Buchanan | American | 1939– |
| Kate Gallison | American | 1939– |
| Sue Grafton | American | 1940– |
| Sara Paretsky | American | 1947– |
| Nevada Barr | American | 1952– |
| Patricia Cornwell | American | 1956– |
| Carol Higgins Clark | American | 1956– |
| Megan Rust | American | 1957– |

It will be seen that their lives span the 20th century. The experiences of these authors, to a greater or lesser degree, are reflected in their writing.

# 1

# Dora Turnbull
## *(Patricia Wentworth)*

Dora Amy Elles, who wrote as Patricia Wentworth in the 20th century, was born in 1878 in Mussoorie, at the foothills of the Himalayas. The daughter of Lt. General Sir Edmund Roche Elles, she began life the year after Queen Victoria was proclaimed Empress of India. The year of her birth coincided with establishment of Scotland Yard's C.I.D.

Dora and her two brothers were brought by their parents to England to live with a grandmother. Later, Dora attended Blackheath High School for Girls in London. Returning to India, she married Lt. Col. George Dillon. After his death in 1906, she took up residence in England, bringing her three stepsons with her.

Dillon's first work had appeared in a newspaper read by the British Raj in the Punjab. Her literary career began in earnest with the writing of *A Marriage Under Terror* (1910), a romance of the French Revolution. It not only won an open prize of about $400 for a first novel, but scored immediate success and was used as textbook for students. By 1927, she had published 15 more books, some of them romances, some romantic thrillers and some verse.

When in her early 40s, Dillon married another military man, Lt. Col. George Oliver Turnbull, who appeared to support her writing with enthusiasm. The couple had one daughter and lived in Surrey.

Although Turnbull's pre–1928 works were well received, her reputation comes from the creation of Miss Silver, first introduced in *The Grey Mask* (1928). However, this lady did not appear again until 1937, although Patricia had written 16 non-series novels in the intervening time.

**Dora Turnbull. Copied by Mary Frey from a photograph in *Twentieth-Century Authors*, First Supplement, 1955.**

Thirty of the Miss Silver series appeared between 1937 and 1961. These books became so popular in the United States that they were published by J.B. Lippincott in Philadelphia before the British editions came out.

A short series about Inspector Ernest Lamb was published between 1939 and 1942. The character is not as well developed as Miss Silver, although the story lines hold the reader's attention. Frank Abbott, who comes to have some importance in the Miss Silver series, is introduced in the Inspector Lamb series. Lamb also appears in the Silver series.

Turnbull claimed that it was her aim to portray ordinary, convincing human characters in extraordinary circumstances. Regarding her best known creation, she wrote: "Miss Silver, who knits her way through one mystery after another and flavours detection with moral maxims, is quite unlike any one else in this field and has become a favourite." Despite her considerable literary success, Turnbull avoided publicity. She kept pet dachshunds, and listed her recreations as reading, gardening, music and motoring. She continued to live in Surrey until her death in 1961.

The elderly Miss Maud Silver remains an appealing character. She was described as small, resembling the governess in some old photographic group. A pince-nez was held by a thin gold chain looped from the side of her bodice. She was also dowdy. Her dress, on one occasion, was "permanently out of date." As late as 1953, she wore a hairnet. She favored a black felt hat in winter and a straw one in summer. But she liked to sport a pin-on watch, a fur tippet, and a bog oak brooch in the form of a rose with a pearl at the center.

After spending 20 years in what she referred to as "the scholastic profession," she became "a private enquiring agent"—"a sleuthess" according to the police. For her efforts, which were remarkably successful, she received remuneration sufficient to enable her to have her own apartment at 15 Montague Mansions S.W. in London and to employ a female factotum named Hannah Meadows.

The author's description of her sleuth's preparation for bed gives some insight into her chief character:

> Miss Silver's neatly curled fringe was controlled by day by an almost invisible hairnet; it was her practice to substitute at night a stronger net. Her blue dressing gown was trimmed with handmade crochet while her black felt slippers boasted blue tufts. Using her bedside lamp, it was her habit to read a passage of Scripture before she fell asleep. Tonight the psalm of her selection [Psalm 27] contained a verse she considered most appropriate and an expression of her trust in what she termed Providence. It ran: "When the wicked, even my enemies and my foes, came upon me to eat up my flesh, they stumbled and fell." She read on, closed the book, laid it down. She switched off the bedside lamp and passed into her usual calm and healthful slumber.

Miss Silver's clients were often obtained by word of mouth. She enjoyed good relations with the police, who sometimes requested her help.

Among them was Chief Inspector Frank Abbott, who remembered her as his governess.

The locale of the stories was sometimes London—*Ladies' Bane* has an excellent description of a young woman lost in a thick London fog—but often she was called to or happened to be visiting in a small English village a few hours by train from London.

Miss Silver informed her clients, "I can take no case with any other object than that of discovering the truth." Her motto was, "Trust me all in all, or not at all." She knew that Tennyson was out of date, but she admired him, and quoted him frequently.

She knitted while she listened to people. The four children of her niece seemed to be the beneficiaries of her activity in this direction. She often coughed "discreetly," according to the book jacket of one of her works.

She has been called "a teacup lady." Her world, for the most part, revolved around upper middle-class English people. About one murderer, the lady sleuth made this observation: "She has an implacable pride of race, a passion amounting to idolatry for her family, its traditions, its exploits, its accumulated possessions." Most of Miss Silver's friends, acquaintances and clients had independent means; one of them spoke for many when she said, "I'm not trained for anything." Yet there are references that keep the various stories contemporary: in a 1954 book, for example, a character says, "We have a National Health Service Act." The National Health Services Act was passed in 1946, years after Miss Silver made her appearance.

Her professional success could be attributed to various factors, her "unflagging interest in people" for one. According to Chief Inspector Lamb: "...people like talking, but they don't like talking to the police. That's where Miss Silver comes in." Chief Constable Randel Marsh explained her real value in arriving at the truth, "She knows people. All the things they hide behind—appearance, manners, the show they are about to put up to prevent people knowing too much about us—she sees right through them and judges you on what's left."

Even after Dora Turnbull concentrated on writing mysteries, she managed to retain romance in her stories. Judging by the number of Miss Silver books that have been reprinted and continue to circulate, her readers like the combination.

## *Listing of Works by Dora Turnbull*

PSEUDONYM: Patricia Wentworth (used throughout)

---

### MISS MAUD SILVER SERIES

*Grey Mask* . . . . . . . . . . 1928
*The Case Is Closed* . . . . . . . . . . 1937
*Lonesome Road* . . . . . . . . . . 1939
*In the Balance* . . . . . . . . . . 1941
(published in England as *Danger Point*)
*The Chinese Shawl* . . . . . . . . . . 1943
*Miss Silver Deals in Death* . . . . . . . . . . 1943
(published in England as *Miss Silver Intervenes*)
*The Clock Strikes Twelve* . . . . . . . . . . 1944
*The Key* . . . . . . . . . . 1944
*She Came Back* . . . . . . . . . . 1945
(published in England as *The Traveller Returns*)
*Pilgrim's Rest* . . . . . . . . . . 1946
(also published as *Dark Threat*)
*Latter End* . . . . . . . . . . 1947
*Wicked Uncle* . . . . . . . . . . 1947
(published in England as *The Spotlight*)
*The Case of William Smith* . . . . . . . . . . 1948
*The Eternity Ring* . . . . . . . . . . 1948
*Miss Silver Comes to Stay* . . . . . . . . . . 1948
*The Catherine Wheel* . . . . . . . . . . 1949
*The Brading Collection* . . . . . . . . . . 1950
(published in England as *Mr. Brading's Collection*)
*Through the Wall* . . . . . . . . . . 1950
*The Ivory Dagger* . . . . . . . . . . 1951
*Anna, Where Are You?* . . . . . . . . . . 1951
(also published as *Death at Deep End*)
*The Watersplash* . . . . . . . . . . 1951
*Ladies' Bane* . . . . . . . . . . 1952
*Out of the Past* . . . . . . . . . . 1953
*Vanishing Point* . . . . . . . . . . 1953
*The Benevent Treasure* . . . . . . . . . . 1954
*The Silent Pool* . . . . . . . . . . 1954
*The Listening Eye* . . . . . . . . . . 1955
*The Fingerprint* . . . . . . . . . . 1956
*The Gazebo* . . . . . . . . . . 1956
(also published as *The Summerhouse*)
*Poison in the Pen* . . . . . . . . . . 1957
*The Alington Inheritance* . . . . . . . . . . 1958
*The Girl in the Cellar* . . . . . . . . . . 1961

## Inspector Ernest Lamb Series

*The Blind Side* . . . . . . . . . . 1939
*Who Pays the Piper?* . . . . . . . . . . 1940
(also published as *Account Rendered*)
*Pursuit of a Parcel* . . . . . . . . . . 1944

## Novels

*Marriage Under the Terror* . . . . . . . . . . 1910
*A Little More than Kin*
(published in the U.S. as *More Than Kin*) . . . . . . . . . . 1911
*The Devil's Wind* . . . . . . . . . . 1912
*The Fire Within* . . . . . . . . . . 1913
*Simon Heriot* . . . . . . . . . . 1914
*Queen Anne Is Dead* . . . . . . . . . . 1915

## Other Crime Novels

*The Astonishing Adventure of Jane Smith* . . . . . . . . . . 1923
*The Annam Jewel* . . . . . . . . . . 1924
*The Red Lacquer Case* . . . . . . . . . . 1924
*The Black Cabinet* . . . . . . . . . . 1925
*The Dower House Mystery* . . . . . . . . . . 1925
*The Amazing Chance* . . . . . . . . . . 1926
*Anne Belinda* . . . . . . . . . . 1927
*Hue and Cry* . . . . . . . . . . 1927
*Will-o-the-Wisp* . . . . . . . . . . 1928
*Fool Errant* . . . . . . . . . . 1929
*Beggar's Choice* . . . . . . . . . . 1930
*The Coldstone* . . . . . . . . . . 1930
*Kingdom Lost* . . . . . . . . . . 1930
*Danger Calling* . . . . . . . . . . 1931
*Nothing Venture* . . . . . . . . . . 1932
*Red Danger* . . . . . . . . . . 1932
(published in the U.S. as *Red Shadow*)
*Seven Green Stones* . . . . . . . . . . 1933
(published in the U.S. as *Outrageous Fortune*)
*Walk with Care* . . . . . . . . . . 1933
*Fear by Night* . . . . . . . . . . 1934
*Devil-in-the-Dark* . . . . . . . . . . 1934
(published in the U.S. as *Touch and Go*)
*Blindfold* . . . . . . . . . . 1935
*Red Stefan* . . . . . . . . . . 1935
*Dead or Alive* . . . . . . . . . . 1936
*Hole and Corner* . . . . . . . . . . 1936
*Down Under* . . . . . . . . . . 1937

*Run!* . . . . . . . . . . 1938
*Rolling Stone* . . . . . . . . . . 1940
*Unlawful Occasions* . . . . . . . . . . 1941
(published in the U.S. as *Weekend with Death*)
*Silence in Court* . . . . . . . . . . 1945

## Poetry

*A Child's Rhyme Book* . . . . . . . . . . 1910
*Beneath the Hunter's Moon: Poems* . . . . . . . . . . 1945
*The Pool of Dreams: Poems* . . . . . . . . . . 1953

## Other

*Earl or Chieftain? The Romance of Hugh O'Neill* . . . . . . . . . . 1919

# 2

# Agatha Christie

Isaac Asimov believed her to be the best mystery writer of all time, and he is not alone in making this estimate of Agatha Christie.

The daughter of Frederick Alvah Miller and Clarissa Margaret (Boehmer), she was born on September 15, 1890, at Ashfield, the spacious home of her parents in Torquay, Devonshire, England. She was given the name of Agatha May Clarissa Miller. Her American father lived on inherited money, spending much of his time entertaining or visiting friends at his cricket club or elsewhere. He and his wife, who were cousins, were happily married; Agatha and her older brother and sister spent a pleasant childhood in a Victorian environment, where, of course, class distinction existed. Torquay was a prosperous spa to which the privileged came for health reasons; it was also a center of culture with a cosmopolitan atmosphere. Young Agatha—a shy child with an unusual imagination—received a permissive education, being taught by her parents and various governesses.

Torquay was noted as a seaside resort, so Mrs. Miller often took Agatha to the beach, where bathing "machines" provided privacy for changing clothes. (Mixed bathing was by then permitted.) Bathing remained one of the joys of Agatha's long life. Also, great was her excitement when she was given Toby, a Yorkshire terrier puppy, for her fifth birthday. He would be the first of her many dogs.

For a family that used lace mats on dessert plates, finger bowls and the like, servants were needed; in fact, the smooth running of Ashfield depended on the efficiency of low-paid domestics and gardeners. Agatha became familiar with these people at an early age, developing a real affection for her nursemaid in particular.

When Agatha was six, her family spent some months in France.

Renting Ashfield was a means of securing much needed income, and living in France was comparatively cheap. It also provided Agatha with the opportunity to learn to speak French.

Frederick Miller died when Agatha was 11, leaving a disconsolate family. Since their financial situation was precarious, economy was necessary. Madge, the older daughter, had been away at school, and soon married. Monty, her brother, had been at Harrow and later was posted to Army duty in India. As time went by, Agatha and her mother, probably because of being together so much without the other two in the family, became exceptionally close.

Agatha sometimes visited her great aunt in Ealing. Known as "Auntie-Granny" because she had raised Mr. Miller, this woman and her Victorian home remained in Agatha's memory. Agatha also remembered visits to Ashfield by Granny B. (for Boehmer), Mrs. Miller's mother. In 1902, Agatha became acquainted with Nan Watts, a sister of her new brother-in-law. Nan came from a rich Manchester family and lived in a large mansion named Abney Hall, where Agatha was often a guest. The two girls struck up a lasting friendship.

Agatha had bathing in summer, roller skating in winter; sometimes she rode—always sidesaddle. And she had many books to read. She and her mother read aloud Scott, Dickens, Dumas, and other authors. *Bleak House* remained a favorite with the girl who would one day write fiction herself. The pair also enjoyed the theater.

By 1906, Mrs. Miller had decided that her daughter must study in Paris. The two winters and one summer that Agatha spent there were memorable and happy. She was exposed to a variety of subjects, but concentrated on singing and piano. Her command of written French improved greatly; she also became convinced that her voice was not strong enough for opera and that her continuing tendency to stage fright would be a serious detriment to such a career.

Next on Mrs. Miller's agenda for her daughter was a stay of three months in Cairo, where 17-year-old Agatha could meet eligible young men. These were British army officers posted in that city. According to Agatha, she went to five dances every week: "...I was passionately fond of dancing and I danced well. I liked young men, and I soon found they liked me, so everything went well." She stated in her autobiography that she was thin and good-looking. She was also abnormally shy, but she had a good sense of humor. In Cairo she developed a great interest in polo. Through her father, she had earlier become a cricket enthusiast.

Around this time, she began to write poetry. *The Poetry Review* published one of her works, and she won several prizes.

Agatha Christie in 1932 by Bessano. By courtesy of the Portrait Gallery, London.

May 19, 1911, was a landmark day in her life. She took an airplane ride that lasted for all of five minutes—and was "wonderful."

Her description of pre–1914 garden parties gave a glimpse at the world in which Agatha moved. Everyone wore high-heeled shoes, muslin dresses with blue sashes, and large leghorn hats with drooping roses. There was ice cream in a variety of flavors—for example, strawberry, vanilla, pistachio; also every kind of cream cake, of sandwich, of éclair. Peaches, muscat grapes and nectarines were offered. Transportation to a garden party was by carriage, hired or otherwise, or by foot, for it was not unusual for young persons to walk, often uphill, for a distance of a mile and a half to two miles.

At her mother's suggestion, Agatha began to write stories. Madge had earlier stimulated her sister's interest in detective stories, and Agatha had resolved that some day she would write one. Madge had even had some success at publication, and it was her typewriter that Agatha used.

Agatha's first attempts met with rejections. She next tried a novel set in Cairo, *Snow Upon the Desert*. Through a family friend who was an author, she was referred to Hughes Massie, a literary agent. Massie said he could not sell the manuscript, but advised her to write another book.

Meanwhile, several men wanted to marry Christie. The one who won her was handsome Archie Christie of the Royal Flying Corps. He was 23, a year older than she, and had less money than Mrs. Miller thought desirable.

When England declared war in 1914, Archie left for France. Agatha became a Volunteer Aid Detachment nurse in a Torquay hospital that cared for the military. It was a converted Town Hall. She enjoyed nursing and considered it one of the most rewarding professions that anyone can follow.

Agatha and Archie were married on Christmas Eve, 1914. With very short leave, he had to return the next day. (Some Britons had believed in August, when war was declared, that the fighting would be over by Christmas.) Christie continued to work at the hospital, but for some weeks was incapacitated by flu.

When she recovered, she had a new job that would last for the next two years. She was assigned to the dispensary, with the anticipation that she would study for the Apothecaries Hall Examination, which would qualify her to dispense drugs. It was arranged that a pharmacist in Torquay give her some instruction.

During her dispensary days, Christie decided to write a detective story, an idea she had had in her mind since discussion with Madge. During slack times at the hospital, she gave it much thought. Though familiar with Sherlock Holmes, she strove to invent a detective of her own, and he would have a Doctor Watson. This was her thinking: "The whole point of a *good* detective story was that it must be somebody obvious but at the same time, for some reason, you would then find that it was *not* obvious, that he could not possibly have done it." She decided against basing her character on real people: "You must create your characters for yourself. Someone you see in a tram or a train or a restaurant is a possible starting point, because you can make up something for yourself about them."

In developing the detective, she remembered Belgian refugees who were living in nearby Tor. Her character was to have had experience in police work. "I could see him as a tidy little man, always arranging things, liking things in pairs, liking things square instead of round. And he could be very brainy—and he should have little grey cells of the mind—that was a good phrase: I must remember that—yes, he would have little grey cells. He would have rather a grand name...." For the latter, she settled on Hercule Poirot. She finished *The Mysterious Affair at Styles* in 1916. It was rejected by the first publisher to whom it was submitted and later by several others. Christie then sent the manuscript to the Bodley Head.

Towards the end of the war, Archie was posted to the Air Ministry in London. Almost four years of service in France had brought him many honors. The couple moved to London, where Agatha took a course in shorthand and bookkeeping. Then suddenly the war was over, with many demobilized men looking for work.

In 1920, *The Mysterious Affair at Styles* was published. Involved in the uncertainties of house hunting in London and the excitement of having daughter Rosalind, Christie had forgotten about the manuscript submitted to the Bodley Head—a manuscript that they ultimately accepted with a small change. She wrote later: "I had some nice reviews for *The Mysterious Affair at Styles*, but the one which pleased me most appeared in *The Pharmaceutical Journal.* It praised the detective story for dealing with poisons in a knowledgeable way, and not with the nonsense about untraceable substances that so often appear. 'Miss Agatha Christie,' they said, 'knows her job.'" Later she would say, "I know nothing about pistols and revolvers, which is why I usually kill off my characters with a blunt instrument—or better still with poisons...."

In accordance with the terms of her contract, she made other submissions to the Bodley Head. The first of these was *The Secret Adversary* (1922), a spy thriller that introduced Tommy and Terrence Beresford. *Murder on the Links* (1923) followed with Hercule Poirot again and his Watson, Captain Arthur Hastings. Christie wrote that the book was probably influenced by a French novel, *Mystery of the Yellow Room*, which she enjoyed.

When the British Empire Mission, which was promoting an exhibition to be held in London in 1924, hired Archie for a round-the-world trip by ship, Agatha accompanied him. The baby and her nurse were sent to Mrs. Miller's home. The nurse and a maid were, according to Christie, essentials of life in those days.

Christie found the trip very exciting, although she suffered from seasickness. The latter was a small price to pay for such events as surfing in Hawaii.

Her writing career was going well—for example, *The Sketch* wanted a series of stories about Poirot, and some of her works were printed in installments. Christie had thought that the public would be more receptive to a detective story writer with a man's name that a woman's. Her publisher, on the other hand, guessed correctly that "Agatha Christie" was distinctive enough to become known as a name. *The Man in the Brown Suit* (1924) was also a success. Nevertheless, Christie had decided to break away from the Bodley Head when the terms of her contract were fulfilled.

When 1925 ended, her publisher was William Collins. Her agent was Edmund Cork, who would prove to be a true friend. The first book for the new publisher was *The Murder of Roger Ackroyd* (1926). It was controversial because there were complaints that it did not conform to the regulation laid down by the elite Detection Club in London that every clue to the identity of the criminal must be placed fairly before the reader. As a member of the Detection Club, Agatha's defense was that her story contained "nothing but the truth though not the whole truth." *Roger Ackroyd* firmly established Christie's career and is still considered a first-class mystery. Her brother-in-law had contributed an idea for it by saying, "What I would like to see is a Watson who turned out to be a criminal." In addition, Lord Louis Mountbatten had written to suggest that a story should be narrated in the first person by someone who later turned out to be the murderer.

Archie had found a position he liked; they went to live in Sunningdale, "in the country," from which he could commute to the city. His wife's earnings enabled the couple to buy a car. Archie became more and more engrossed in golf. Agatha had secretarial help with her writing, which was absorbing more and more of her time.

Christie gave information about herself that helps the reader to understand the author. In her own words: "I can't say what I mean easily—I can write it better." She knew she could write; she admitted to being a reasonable musician, but not a professional; she could improvise. She did not like crowds; she disliked smoking and drinking. She liked sunshine, apples, almost any kind of music, railway trains, numerical puzzles, swimming, eating, most dogs, and going to the theater.

Clarissa Miller died in 1926, leaving Christie devastated. In the summer of that year, Archie asked her for a divorce; he wanted to marry an attractive golf companion named Nancy Neele. The two events seemed to affect Agatha's mental health. On December 3, 1926, she drove away from Styles, the home named in honor of her first book.

The next day her car was found abandoned on the edge of a pond. The success of *Roger Ackroyd* had made its author famous, and an extensive search was organized. Suspecting suicide, the authorities dragged the pond. No body was found. Meanwhile, a Mrs. Teresa Neele had checked into a spa resort in Harrogate, Yorkshire. Bob Tappin, greengrocer by day and banjo player and singer in the hotel's band, informed the police that Mrs. Neele resembled the newspaper photos of the missing author. He had become fascinated by the good-looking woman with golden-red hair and blue eyes who borrowed detective books from the hotel library. On December 14, Archie identified Mrs. Neele as Agatha Christie. Neele was the last name of his paramour.

Two doctors declared officially that "[Mrs. Agatha Christie] is suffering from an unquestionable loss of memory...." Many people doubted that Agatha had amnesia. Much speculation was made, but the matter remains a mystery.

Christie's alleged amnesia was treated by a psychiatrist who used hypnosis. Because of recent events and a prying press, she yearned to leave England for a short period. (At this point she took an anti-publicity stand.) She satisfied her desire by taking Rosalind and Carlo to the Canary Islands. Carlo was the nickname of Carol Fisher, who doubled as Christie's secretary and Rosalind's governess. During that period, she managed to work on a book, although she had to contend with interruptions by her daughter. Christie noted later that during that time, she became a professional, writing when she was not so inclined, but getting the job done.

Back in England a few months later, she moved to a small house in London. She reluctantly granted Archie a divorce. Rosalind went to boarding school, leaving the loyal Carlo with more time to help Christie.

She had some free time before Christmas that year. Making a quick decision, she took the Orient Express to Baghdad. This was her first experience traveling alone, and in a way, she welcomed her new independence. She relished the journey, which had stops at Paris, Lucerne, Milan, Venice, Trieste, Zagret, Belgrade, Sophia, and Istanbul. On this trip, she met the renowned archeologist Leonard Wooley and his wife, who invited Christie to visit them at Ur in the Near East, the scene of archeological diggings. Here she met Leonard Wooley's assistant, Max Mallowan. He was delegated to show her various sights, and the two had good opportunity to become well acquainted. Although Max was 14 years younger than Agatha, they married in Edinburgh in 1930. Christie had also brought up the fact that he was a Catholic and she an Anglican; neither age nor religion differences seemed to bother Max. The union proved to be a very happy one, though childless. (Christie had one miscarriage.)

Max taught at Oxford for part of each year, so they bought a house between Oxford and London. He was involved in annual diggings, and Agatha went with him. Genuinely interested in his work, she became his competent photographer.

She did not neglect her writing: between 1929 and 1932; two collections of short stories were published in addition to her books. Of the latter, she produced one or two a year—in fact, there was soon in the book world the expectation of "a Christie for Christmas." This required a March delivery of the manuscript to the publisher. Agatha did not care for any editing of her text and wanted to have a say in anything related to her books.

The first book in which Miss Jane Marple appeared was *Murder in the Vicerage* (1930). Although an amateur, this lady would become almost as famous a detective as Poirot. Christie was beginning to see significant financial returns. When her new mother-in-law suggested that she should be writing something more *serious*, Agatha did not reply. Apparently she found it difficult to explain conversationally that her intent was to write for entertainment. At this time, her requirements for writing space and equipment were simple. "All I needed was a sturdy table and a typewriter," she wrote, "though I still used to do the beginning chapters and occasionally others in longhand, and then type them out." The sturdy table was a must, even when she was living under primitive conditions in Iraq. According to Max, his wife always wrote the last chapter of a book first. He also divulged that Agatha's character, Mrs. Ariadne Oliver, was based on his wife.

The years between 1930 and 1938 were particularly satisfying to Christie "because they were so free of outside shadows." She spent summers at Ashfield and acquired nearby Greenway House. Admitting that houses were her passion, she explained in her autobiography that not long before the outbreak of World War II, she was the proud possessor of eight homes.

With the advent of the war, Max joined the Air Ministry, which loaned him to the British military government in North Africa. To put his knowledge of Arabic to use, he was made an adviser on Arab affairs. Agatha again used her dispensing training on behalf of her country by working at University College Hospital in London—two whole days and three half-days a week as well as alternate Saturday mornings. The rest of the time she wrote—continuing to turn out publishable material. Here is her description of the bombings:

> It had become, in fact, natural to expect that you yourself might be killed soon, that the people you loved best might be killed, that you would hear of the deaths of friends. Broken windows, bombs, land mines, and in due course flying bombs and rockets—all these things would go on, not as something extraordinary, but as perfectly natural. After three years of war, they were an everyday happening. You could not really envisage a time when there would not be a war any more.

The war made changes in Christie's life. Rosalind married Herbert Prichard, a major in the regular British Army. Mathew, Christie's grandson and great joy, was born in 1943. His father was killed later. Greenway, a favorite home of the Mallowans, was taken over by the British Admiralty—for use by American services.

In 1949, important diggings were begun at Nimrud (the ancient city known as Calah) in Iraq. Under Max's supervision, the project continued for 10 years and brought him fame. The Mallowans maintained a home in Baghdad for many years. It was at Nimrud in 1950 that Christie began her autobiography. She finished it in 1965, but at the request of this private woman, it was not published until 1977, after her death.

As the years went by, Agatha and Max enjoyed Greenway more and more, entertaining many guests there. She was thankful that the Americans, who had occupied it during the war years, had cared for it so well. In the post-war period, Rosalind married Anthony Hicks.

Before she died, Agatha wrote, in addition to mysteries and thrillers, miscellaneous books, including: romances, poetry, reminisces, a children's book, her autobiography and 21 plays. Her novels were written under the pseudonym of Mary Westmacott. She was outsold only by the Bible and Shakespeare. She received poor marks for political correctness—for example, when loaning money was under discussion, this sentence appeared: "I suspect a Semitic strain in their ancestry." Her narratives, however, show much of the interests of the day—mah jong in 1926, spiritualism in 1933, a new drug for tuberculosis in 1953, and so on.

Detective story writer H.F.R. Keeting summed up Christie's literary ability with: "She never tried to be clever in her writing, only ingenious in her plots. She knew, too, from the sympathy she had for ordinary people, at just what moment they needed each piece of information to build up the story she was telling. She served her public."

Late in life, when asked why she was not interested in modern fiction, she answered:

As I grow older and older
And totter towards the tomb
I find that I care less and less
Who goes to bed with whom

Although popular with the reading public, Christie was not always praised by the critics, among them Edmund Wilson. He wrote, "...her writing is of mawkishness and banality which seems to me literally impossible to read."

When the British Broadcasting Corporation requested a short radio play to honor Queen Mary's birthday, Christie provided a half-hour production entitled *Three Blind Mice.* From this evolved the stage play she named *The Mousetrap.* The title was suggested by her son-in-law. She said he should have shared in the royalties. He did not, because she had arranged to have them go to grandson Mathew, age eight at that time. This gave him a fortune, since *The Mousetrap* became the longest continuously running stage play in history. Thanks to producer Peter Saunders, the play became a tourist attraction for Americans visiting in London. *Witness for the Prosecution* (1953) was another highly successful play. *Ten Little Niggers* (1943) was adapted for the stage from the 1939 novel with the same title. (It opened in New York City in 1944 with the title *Ten Little Indians.* In an era of political correctness, that too probably would not be acceptable. In 1944, it was presumably an improvement on *Ten Little Niggers.)* There have been many movie adaptations of Christie works, most of them not popular with the author. Successes included *And Then There Were None/Ten Little Niggers* (1945), *Witness for the Prosecution* (1957) and *Murder on the Orient Express* (1947).

Readers may be familiar with two British television series that presented Christie's most famous characters. One series featured David Suchet as Poirot and another featured Joan Hickson as Miss Marple.

Christie's advice to aspiring writers was, "If you really want to write you must decide what kind of style you want to work in and then read books that have the same style." She warned that the rejections of books and magazine articles is very depressing. Contending that everything in life is partly hard work and partly luck, she stated, "And luck is really the important thing."

*The Agatha Christie Companion* by Dennis Sanders and Len Lovallo is an excellent guide to her works.

Besides receiving great financial returns from her writing, Christie was honored by her country. In 1956, she became Champion of the British Empire, and in 1971, Dame of the British Empire. In 1961, the University of Exeter conferred on her the LL.D. degree. She was also awarded, in 1954, the first Grand Master Award of the Mystery Writers of America. MALICE DOMESTIC, a convention established in 1989, gives Agatha awards in honor of Christie.

Another Mallowan was recognized: four years after Agatha, Max was granted a C.B.E. for his archeological findings, and in 1968, he was knighted.

For her 80th birthday, Christie's publisher gave her a Dictaphone, which she found exceptionally useful because she had broken a wrist.

In 1971 she suffered a broken hip, which friends thought hastened her decline. *Postern of Fate* (1973) was the last book she wrote. By 1975, it was realized that there would be no Christie for Christmas. There was however, a final gathering at her home in Wallingford. Dame Agatha Christie Mallowan died on January 12, 1976, at the age of 85. At a memorial service in St. Martin's-in-the-Fields, Sir William Collins, her publisher for so many years, said, "...she possessed in supreme measure one mark of literary greatness, the art of telling a story."

As noted previously, Christie used her pharmacological knowledge in her fiction. Her world-wide travels were also reflected in her short stories and books. Examples of the latter are *Murder on the Orient Express* (1934), *Murder in Mesopotamia* (1936), *Death in the Nile* (1939) and *A Caribbean Mystery* (1964).

The most telling influence was Christie's upper middle class background. Born at a time when women of her social stratum did not ordinarily have careers, she showed little interest in feminism. She did like to write what came to be known as "cozy" mysteries, usually set in a village or the countryside, and not concerned with burning issues.

Her most memorable creation was Hercule Poirot. As mentioned, he was a retired Belgian police officer. As she used him over more and more years, she regretted that he had been elderly when she first presented him. This gentleman was short, dignified and very neat, dressing with sartorial perfection; distinguishing characteristics were his egg-shaped head and his stiff military mustache. He admitted to enjoying "the pleasures of the table," which included hot chocolate. Since Christie considered a love interest in her stories a bore, Poirot had no romance in his life. Agatha put him on stage as a wise and experienced detective who could work well with Chief Inspector James Japp and his like. Skilled in psychology, Poirot claimed that it was always *people* that interested him. Here is his reasoning in *Third Girl* (1966): "What did he feel about the case?—What kind of a case was it? Let him start from the general, then proceed to the particular. What were the salient facts of this case?... Half these facts are irrelevant. I want a pattern. A pattern. My kingdom for a pattern."

Poirot appeared in 38 full-length novels and collections of short stories. The last book was *Curtain*, written many years before its publication in 1975. The news that the aging crime writer had killed off her famous detective elicited front-page coverage by *The New York Times* of August 6, 1975.

Miss Marple was also brought in to help the police solve difficult cases. An aged spinster, she was tall, thin and blue-eyed. Her residence was the fictional village of St. Mary Mead. Here is Inspector Neale's estimate of this Victorian lady who spent much of her time knitting: "She was upright, of unspeakable rectitude and she had, like most old ladies, time on her hands and an old maid's nose for scenting bits of gossip." Miss Marple operated on the principle that human nature is the same everywhere and that the common-sense explanation "is so often right." She had respect for the police and her viewpoint that "the wicked should not go unpunished" mirrored Agatha's publicly expressed sentiments. Miss Marple was disposed of in *Sleeping Murder*, published in 1976, but like *Curtain*, completed years earlier. Shaw and Vanaker pointed out that Miss Marple represented logic, morality and justice. There is a similarity between the geriatric sleuths, Miss Silver and her contemporary, Miss Marple. According to H.R.F. Keating, both were created in 1928, neither deriving from the other.

Christie noted that she had endowed Miss Marple "with something of Grannie's powers of prophecy" and that the lady from St. Mary Mead was rather like some of her grandmother's cronies in Ealing. Miss Marple's creator also wrote: "I think it is possible that [she] arose from the pleasure I had in portraying Dr. Sheppard's sister in *The Murder of Roger Ackroyd.* She had been my favorite character in the book—an acidulated spinster, full of curiosity, knowing everything, hearing everything; the complete detective service in the house."

Hercule Poirot and Jane Marple certainly are not 21st-cemtury characters, nor is the world they frequent—a world of servants, inherited money, leisure time, exotic places and so on. Yet Christie's writings continue to appeal to readers. The latest edition of *Books in Print* (Authors) has columns of Christie titles. Charles Osborne adapted as novels the Christie plays *Black Coffee* and *The Unexpected Guest*, popular decades before. And so it goes. Dame Agatha Christie must have understood the art of creating timeless appeal for her readership.

## *Listing of Works by Agatha Christie*

PSEUDONYMS: Mary Westmacott, Agatha Mallowan

### HERCULE POIROT SERIES

*The Mysterious Affair at Styles* . . . . . . . . . . 1920
*The Murder on the Links* . . . . . . . . . . 1923
*The Murder of Roger Ackroyd* . . . . . . . . . . 1926
*The Big Four* . . . . . . . . . . 1927
*The Mystery of the Blue Train* . . . . . . . . . . 1928
*Peril at End House* . . . . . . . . . . 1932
*Thirteen at Dinner* . . . . . . . . . . 1933
(published in England as *Lord Edgware Dies*)
*Murder in Three Acts* . . . . . . . . . . 1934
(published in England as *Three Act Tragedy*)
*Murder on the Calais Coach* . . . . . . . . . . 1934
(published in England as *Murder on the Orient Express*)
*Death in the Air* . . . . . . . . . . 1935
(published in England as *Death in the Clouds*)
*The A. B. C. Murders* . . . . . . . . . . 1935
(also published as *The Alphabet Murders*)
*Cards on the Table* . . . . . . . . . . 1936
*Murder in Mesopotamia* . . . . . . . . . . 1936
*Death on the Nile* . . . . . . . . . . 1937
*Poirot Loses a Client* . . . . . . . . . . 1937
(published in England as *Dumb Witness*)
*Appointment with Death* . . . . . . . . . . 1938
*Hercule Poirot's Christmas* . . . . . . . . . . 1938
(also published as *Murder for Christmas* and as *A Holiday for Murder*)
*One, Two, Buckle My Shoe* . . . . . . . . . . 1940
(also published as *The Patriotic Murders* and as *An Overdose of Death*; reprinted as *The Patriotic Murders*)
*Sad Cypress* . . . . . . . . . . 1940
*Evil Under the Sun* . . . . . . . . . . 1941
*Murder in Retrospect* . . . . . . . . . . 1942
(published in England as *Five Little Pigs*)
*The Hollow*
(published in the U.S. as *Murder After Hours*) . . . . . . . . . . 1946
*There Is a Tide...* . . . . . . . . . . 1948
(published in England as *Taken at the Flood*)
*Mrs. McGinty's Dead* . . . . . . . . . . 1952
(published as *Blood Will Tell)*
*Funerals Are Fatal* . . . . . . . . . . 1953

(published in England as *After the Funeral*; also published as *Murder at the Gallop*)
*Hickory, Dickory, Death* . . . . . . . . . . . . . . . . . . . . . . . . . . . . . . . . . 1955
(published in England as *Hickory, Dickory, Dock*)
*Dead Man's Folly* . . . . . . . . . . . . . . . . . . . . . . . . . . . . . . . . . . . . 1956
*Cat Among the Pigeons* . . . . . . . . . . . . . . . . . . . . . . . . . . . . . . . 1959
*The Clocks* . . . . . . . . . . . . . . . . . . . . . . . . . . . . . . . . . . . . . . . . 1963
*Third Girl* . . . . . . . . . . . . . . . . . . . . . . . . . . . . . . . . . . . . . . . . 1966
*Hallowe'en Party* . . . . . . . . . . . . . . . . . . . . . . . . . . . . . . . . . . . 1969
*Elephants Can Remember* . . . . . . . . . . . . . . . . . . . . . . . . . . . . . 1972
*Curtain: Hercule Poirot's Last Case* . . . . . . . . . . . . . . . . . . . . . . 1975

### Miss Jane Marple Series

*The Murder at the Vicarage* . . . . . . . . . . . . . . . . . . . . . . . . . . . 1930
*The Body in the Library* . . . . . . . . . . . . . . . . . . . . . . . . . . . . . 1942
*The Moving Finger* . . . . . . . . . . . . . . . . . . . . . . . . . . . . . . . . . 1942
*A Murder Is Announced* . . . . . . . . . . . . . . . . . . . . . . . . . . . . . 1950
*Murder with Mirrors* . . . . . . . . . . . . . . . . . . . . . . . . . . . . . . . 1952
(published in England as *They Do It with Mirrors*)
*A Pocket Full of Rye* . . . . . . . . . . . . . . . . . . . . . . . . . . . . . . . 1953
*What Mrs. McGillicudy Saw* . . . . . . . . . . . . . . . . . . . . . . . . . . 1957
(published in England as *4:50 from Paddington*; also published as *Murder She Said*)
*The Mirror Crack'd from Side to Side* . . . . . . . . . . . . . . . . . . . 1962
(published in the U.S. as *The Mirror Crack'd*)
*A Caribbean Mystery* . . . . . . . . . . . . . . . . . . . . . . . . . . . . . . 1964
*At Bertram's Hotel* . . . . . . . . . . . . . . . . . . . . . . . . . . . . . . . . 1965
(revised edition, 1984)
*Nemesis* . . . . . . . . . . . . . . . . . . . . . . . . . . . . . . . . . . . . . . . . 1971
*Sleeping Murder* . . . . . . . . . . . . . . . . . . . . . . . . . . . . . . . . . 1976

(Miss Jane Marple novels also published in various omnibus volumes)

### Tuppence and Tommy Beresford Series

*The Secret Adversary* . . . . . . . . . . . . . . . . . . . . . . . . . . . . . . 1922
*N or M?* . . . . . . . . . . . . . . . . . . . . . . . . . . . . . . . . . . . . . . . . 1941
*By the Pricking of My Thumbs* . . . . . . . . . . . . . . . . . . . . . . . . 1968
*Postern of Fate* . . . . . . . . . . . . . . . . . . . . . . . . . . . . . . . . . . 1973

### Mystery Novels

*The Man in the Brown Suit* . . . . . . . . . . . . . . . . . . . . . . . . . . 1924
*The Secret of Chimneys* . . . . . . . . . . . . . . . . . . . . . . . . . . . . . 1925

*The Seven Dials Mystery* . . . . . . . . . . . . . . . . . . . . . . . . . . . . 1929
(With others) *The Floating Admiral* . . . . . . . . . . . . . . . . . . . . . 1931
*The Murder at Hazelmoor* . . . . . . . . . . . . . . . . . . . . . . . . . . . . 1931
(published in England as *The Sittaford Mystery*)
*Why Didn't They Ask Evans?* . . . . . . . . . . . . . . . . . . . . . . . . . 1935
(published also as *The Boomerang Club*)
*Easy to Kill* . . . . . . . . . . . . . . . . . . . . . . . . . . . . . . . . . . . . 1939
(published in England as *Murder Is Easy*)
*Ten Little Niggers* . . . . . . . . . . . . . . . . . . . . . . . . . . . . . . . 1939
(published in the U.S. as *And Then There Were None* and as *Ten Little Indians*)
*Death Comes as the End* . . . . . . . . . . . . . . . . . . . . . . . . . . . . 1944
*Towards Zero* . . . . . . . . . . . . . . . . . . . . . . . . . . . . . . . . . . . 1944
*Remembered Death* . . . . . . . . . . . . . . . . . . . . . . . . . . . . . . . 1945
(published in England as *Sparkling Cyanide*)
*The Crooked House* . . . . . . . . . . . . . . . . . . . . . . . . . . . . . . . 1949
*They Came to Baghdad* . . . . . . . . . . . . . . . . . . . . . . . . . . . . . 1951
*Destination Unknown* . . . . . . . . . . . . . . . . . . . . . . . . . . . . . . 1954
(published in the U.S. as *So Many Steps to Death*)
*Ordeal by Innocence* . . . . . . . . . . . . . . . . . . . . . . . . . . . . . . 1958
*The Pale Horse* . . . . . . . . . . . . . . . . . . . . . . . . . . . . . . . . . 1961
*Endless Night* . . . . . . . . . . . . . . . . . . . . . . . . . . . . . . . . . . 1967
*Passenger to Frankfurt* . . . . . . . . . . . . . . . . . . . . . . . . . . . . 1970
*Murder on Board* . . . . . . . . . . . . . . . . . . . . . . . . . . . . . . . . 1974
(With others) *The Scoop* and *Behind the Scenes* . . . . . . . . . . . . . 1983

## Novels as Mary Westmacott

*Giant's Bread* . . . . . . . . . . . . . . . . . . . . . . . . . . . . . . . . . . 1930
*Unfinished Portrait* . . . . . . . . . . . . . . . . . . . . . . . . . . . . . . . 1934
*Absent in the Spring* . . . . . . . . . . . . . . . . . . . . . . . . . . . . . . 1944
*The Rose and the Yew Tree* . . . . . . . . . . . . . . . . . . . . . . . . . . 1948
*A Daughter's a Daughter* . . . . . . . . . . . . . . . . . . . . . . . . . . . 1952
*The Burden* . . . . . . . . . . . . . . . . . . . . . . . . . . . . . . . . . . . . 1956

## Some Short Story Collections

*Poirot Investigates* . . . . . . . . . . . . . . . . . . . . . . . . . . . . . . . 1924
*Partners in Crime* . . . . . . . . . . . . . . . . . . . . . . . . . . . . . . . . 1929
(abridged edition published in England as *The Sunningdale Mystery*)
*The Under Dog, and Other Stories* . . . . . . . . . . . . . . . . . . . . . . 1929
*The Mysterious Mr. Quin* . . . . . . . . . . . . . . . . . . . . . . . . . . . . 1930
(also published as *The Passing of Mr. Quin*)
*The Thirteen Problems* . . . . . . . . . . . . . . . . . . . . . . . . . . . . . 1932
(also published as *The Tuesday Club Murders;* abridged edition published as *The Mystery of the Blue Geraniums, and Other Tuesday Club Murders*)
*The Hound of Death, and Other Stories* . . . . . . . . . . . . . . . . . . . 1933

*The Listerdale Mystery, and Other Stories* . . . . . . . . . . . . . . . . . . . . . . . . . 1934
*Mr. Parker Pyne, Detective* . . . . . . . . . . . . . . . . . . . . . . . . . . . . . . . . 1934
(published in England as *Parker Pyne Investigates*)
*Dead Man's Mirror, and Other Stories* . . . . . . . . . . . . . . . . . . . . . . . . . . 1937
(published in England as *Murder in the Mews, and Three Other Poirot Stories*)
*The Regatta Mystery, and Other Stories* . . . . . . . . . . . . . . . . . . . . . . . . . 1939
*The Mystery of the Baghdad Chest* . . . . . . . . . . . . . . . . . . . . . . . . . . . . 1943
*The Mystery of the Crime in Cabin 66* . . . . . . . . . . . . . . . . . . . . . . . . . 1943
(published in England as *The Crime in Cabin 66)*
*Poirot on Holiday* . . . . . . . . . . . . . . . . . . . . . . . . . . . . . . . . . . . . . 1943
*Poirot and the Regatta Mystery* . . . . . . . . . . . . . . . . . . . . . . . . . . . . . 1943
*Problem at Pollensa Bay* [and] *Christmas Adventure* . . . . . . . . . . . . . . . . 1943
*The Veiled Lady* [and] *The Mystery of the Baghdad Chest* . . . . . . . . . . . . . . 1944
*Poirot Knows the Murderer* . . . . . . . . . . . . . . . . . . . . . . . . . . . . . . . 1946
*Poirot Lends a Hand* . . . . . . . . . . . . . . . . . . . . . . . . . . . . . . . . . . . 1946
*The Labours of Hercules: New Adventures in Crime by Hercule Poirot* . . . . . 1947
*Witness for the Prosecution, and Other Stories* . . . . . . . . . . . . . . . . . . . . 1948
*The Mousetrap, and Other Stories* . . . . . . . . . . . . . . . . . . . . . . . . . . . . 1949
(published as *Three Blind Mice and Other Stories*)
*The Adventure of the Christmas Pudding, and Selection of Entrees* . . . . . . . . 1960
*Double Sin, and Other Stories* . . . . . . . . . . . . . . . . . . . . . . . . . . . . . . 1961
*13 for Luck!: A Selection of Mystery Stories for Young Readers* . . . . . . . . . . . 1961
*Surprise! Surprise!: A Collection of Mystery Stories with Unexpected Endings* . . . . . . . . . . . . . . . . . . . . . . . . . . . . . . . . . . . . . . . . . . 1965
*13 Clues for Miss Marple* . . . . . . . . . . . . . . . . . . . . . . . . . . . . . . . . . 1966
*Selected Stories* . . . . . . . . . . . . . . . . . . . . . . . . . . . . . . . . . . . . . . 1969
*The Golden Ball, and Other Stories* . . . . . . . . . . . . . . . . . . . . . . . . . . . 1971
*Hercule Poirot's Early Cases* . . . . . . . . . . . . . . . . . . . . . . . . . . . . . . . 1974
(published in England as *Poirot's Early Cases*)
*Miss Marple's Final Cases, and Two Other Stories* . . . . . . . . . . . . . . . . . . 1979
*Hercule Poirot's Casebook: Fifty Stories* . . . . . . . . . . . . . . . . . . . . . . . 1984
*The Agatha Christie Hour* . . . . . . . . . . . . . . . . . . . . . . . . . . . . . . . . 1982
*Miss Marple: The Complete Short Stories* . . . . . . . . . . . . . . . . . . . . . . . 1985
(Contributor) *More Murder Most Cozy: More Mysteries in the Classic Tradition* . . . . . . . . . . . . . . . . . . . . . . . . . . . . . . . . . . . . . . . 1993

(There are numerous Agatha Christie omnibus volumes)

### Under the Name Agatha Christie Mallowan

*Star Over Bethlehem, and Other Stories* . . . . . . . . . . . . . . . . . . . . . . . . 1965

### Plays

*Black Coffee* . . . . . . . . . . . . . . . . . . . . . . . . . . . . . . . . . . . . . . . . 1934
*Ten Little Niggers* . . . . . . . . . . . . . . . . . . . . . . . . . . . . . . . . . . . . . 1944

(based on novel of the same title; published in the U.S. as *Ten Little Indians*)
*Appointment with Death* . . . . . . . . . . . . . . . . . . . . . . . . . . . . . . . . 1945
(based on the novel of the same title)
*Little Horizon* . . . . . . . . . . . . . . . . . . . . . . . . . . . . . . . . . . . . 1948
(based on the novel *Death on the Nile*; revised version entitled *Murder on the Nile*)
*The Hollow*
(based on the novel of the same title) . . . . . . . . . . . . . . . . . . . . . . . 1952
*The Mousetrap*
(based on the radio script *Three Blind Mice*) . . . . . . . . . . . . . . . . . . . 1954
*Witness for the Prosecution* . . . . . . . . . . . . . . . . . . . . . . . . . . . . 1954
(based on the short story of the same title)
*Spider's Web* . . . . . . . . . . . . . . . . . . . . . . . . . . . . . . . . . . . . 1957
*The Unexpected Guest* . . . . . . . . . . . . . . . . . . . . . . . . . . . . . . . 1958
*Verdict* . . . . . . . . . . . . . . . . . . . . . . . . . . . . . . . . . . . . . . . 1958
*Go Back for Murder* . . . . . . . . . . . . . . . . . . . . . . . . . . . . . . . . 1960
(based on the novel *Five Little Pigs*)
*Rule of Three* . . . . . . . . . . . . . . . . . . . . . . . . . . . . . . . . . . . . 1963
(contains *Afternoon at the Sea-side, The Patient* and *The Rats*)
*Fiddlers Three* . . . . . . . . . . . . . . . . . . . . . . . . . . . . . . . . . . . 1972
*Akhnaton* . . . . . . . . . . . . . . . . . . . . . . . . . . . . . . . . . . . . . . 1973
*The Mousetrap, and Other Plays* . . . . . . . . . . . . . . . . . . . . . . . . . 1978

## WITH GERALD VERNER

*Towards Zero* . . . . . . . . . . . . . . . . . . . . . . . . . . . . . . . . . . . . 1957
(based on the novel of the same title)

## RADIO PLAYS

*The Mousetrap* . . . . . . . . . . . . . . . . . . . . . . . . . . . . . . . . . . . 1952
(originally broadcast as *Three Blind Mice*, British Broadcasting Corporation [BBC]-Radio)
*Personal Call* . . . . . . . . . . . . . . . . . . . . . . . . . . . . . . . . . . . 1960
BBC-Radio

## OTHER

*The Road of Dreams* (poems) . . . . . . . . . . . . . . . . . . . . . . . . . . . . 1925
*Come, Tell Me How You Live* (autobiographical travel book) . . . . . . . . . . 1946
*Poems* . . . . . . . . . . . . . . . . . . . . . . . . . . . . . . . . . . . . . . . . 1973
(Editor with others) *The Times of London Anthology of Detective Stories* . . 1973
*Agatha Christie: An Autobiography* . . . . . . . . . . . . . . . . . . . . . . . 1977

# 3

# Dorothy L. Sayers

This scholarly woman took great pride in her various academic and religious pursuits. Ironically, she is known to the general public for her creation of Lord Peter Wimsey, amateur sleuth. She needed money, and she once observed that there was a market for detective fiction—that he might go some way towards providing bread and cheese. He did that, and it also became her long-cherished aim to raise the detective story to the level of the novel of manners, as it was in the time of Wilkie Collins. She was one of the writers of detective fiction's Golden Age—the period between the two world wars.

Her numerous letters have been preserved, and much of what is known about her is based on them. Biographies by Brabazon and by Reynolds give many insights.

Dorothy L. Sayers was born in Oxford, England, June 13, 1893, the only child of the Reverend Henry and Helen Mary (Leigh) Sayers. As a minister in the Church of England, Henry Sayers enjoyed a high position in a class-conscious society. At the time of Dorothy's birth, he was headmaster and chaplain to the Choir School of Christ Church College. He was known to love music and books. Her mother was a spirited woman with a distinguished lineage—the reason why her daughter used "L." for Leigh, as part of her professional name. When Dorothy was four, the family moved to the village of Bluntisham, in the Fenns and not far from Cambridge. She left some autobiographical material that gives glimpses of her early life.

Loved by her parents, her childhood was happy, although she was rather isolated from children of her own age. He father read to her Uncle Remus stories, Grimm's fairy tales and the Alice books by Lewis Carroll.

**Dorothy L. Sayers in 1932 by Howard Coster. By courtesy of the National Portrait Gallery, London.**

Her toy monkeys, Jacko and Jocko, were favorites. She was the darling of her Aunt Mabel Leigh and of her Grandmother Sayers. Thanks to instruction at home, she was reading at age four and soon was learning Latin, French and German. Her parents loved the theater and sometimes took her to London to see plays. It was not long until Dorothy was producing plays herself—at 13 she enlisted everyone she could find to act in *The Three Musketeers*. This was just one indication of her creative powers—fiction, drama and poetry would be part of her life. She also played the violin. One memory that remained with her was that of a pony used to pull a two-wheeled conveyance. This particular pony was hard to catch in the paddock, and the Sayers' guests were known to have missed trains because their transport to the station was late. The memory was so impressive that Dorothy used it in one of her books. An early confidant was Ivy Shrimpton, a cousin and five years her senior. In years to come, Ivy would play a major part in Dorothy's life.

The Sayers recognized their daughter's intellect and talent and decided to send her to one of the women's colleges at Oxford. But entrance required a good education, and it became clear that Dorothy would have to go to boarding school. They chose the Godolphin School in Salisbury, more than 100 miles away from their home. She was not happy there and being inept at field hockey added to her woes, but she received the anticipated academic preparation. In 1912, she won the Gilchrist Scholarship to Somerville College. Her father contributed the cost of books, travel and such, as well as a personal allowance.

Although Somerville College was founded in 1879, degrees were not granted to women until 1920. Nevertheless, Dorothy prized her Oxford education, never forgetting that she was a scholar. Witty and fun-loving, she seemed to be popular with a small group of students that called itself the Mutual Admiration Society. Admission required the reading of an original writing at a meeting of the group. In 1916, the dedication to a volume of her poetry summed up what she then believed were her most important Oxford experiences: the joy of comradeship in organizing and directing a play, the glory of singing with the Bach choir, and the creative stimulus of exchanging and discussing poetry with fellow enthusiasts. Her knowledge of academe was reflected in *Gaudy Night.* (Gaudy refers to an annual dinner at a British university.)

In 1915, Dorothy passed examinations that would have given her a first-class degree in modern languages. She could have obtained it quickly by going to Trinity College in Dublin, but she decided to wait until War World I was over, at which time it was expected that Oxford authorities would be enlightened enough to give women official recognition when they had met the requirements.

Britain was facing a shortage of teachers because of the war. When Hull High School for Girls needed a teacher of modern languages, Dorothy was selected. Her heart was not really in teaching; she suffered through Zeppelin raids. But she was earning a living. She continued to write the poetry that had occupied her time for so long. Also, she was having some success at publication. At this period of her life, she began to translate *Tristan* by a French poet.

By now Sayers knew that she wanted to be a writer. Her father was sympathetic to the idea and because he was about to take another parish, was in a position to offer financial aid. The plan was that she would learn publishing as an apprentice to Basil Blackwell, at the same time living in Oxford, where postgraduate work would be possible. She pursued this course for two years, receiving the M.A. at the same time as the B.A. Her writings at this period were not about crime; they showed clearly that religion played an important role in her life. How much her interest was intellectual and how much emotional is difficult to judge. She had leaning towards Catholicism, but remained High Anglican.

Sayers' next venture took her to France in 1919. Ex-Captain Eric Whelpton, whom she knew at Oxford, taught English in a school at Verneuil, about 60 miles from Paris; he also arranged exchanges between British and French schoolboys. Sayers was attracted to him, and welcomed the opportunity to work for him as a secretary of sorts. She could use her French to advantage and sometimes she could get back to London. Whelpton soon fell in love with someone else, making the position less attractive to her. She prepared to leave.

Whelpton wrote later that he believed the figure of a detective was at that time taking shape in Sayer's mind; that this character was based partly on an impoverished British ex-cavalry officer named Charles Crichton whom she had met at Verneuil and on Whelpton himself. The physical characteristics of this detective (Lord Peter Wimsey) mirrored those of another man.

Sayers was sure that being in London among avant-garde friends and acquaintances was the place for an authoress-to-be, certainly preferable to staying with her parents in the rectory at Christchurch, Cambridgeshire. But to do this, she had to accept support from her father.

She began a novel in which Lord Peter made his debut. She also fell in love again. The Russian-born John Cournos was a journalist and poet who had written novels; he was in touch with literary and Bohemian London. His good looks and authoritative manner appealed to Sayers. She wanted to marry him and have children, but he claimed to believe in free love and was resolved never to marry. The upshot was that Cournos left England and in 1924, married a writer with the pseudonym of Sybil Norton. This rejection, added to by that by Whelpton, appears to have hurt Sayers deeply.

In 1922, she had gone to work as a copywriter at the advertising firm of S.H. Benson. It was hardly a job that required her university education, but it did involve one of her fortes—playing with words. She did advertising campaigns for, for example, Coleman and Guinness. The pay was good, and, she found her colleagues stimulating. The position provided an additional bonus—the background for her *Murder Must Advertise* (1933). She was then living in a flat at 24 Great James Street, a residence that she would keep the rest of her life.

The detective story she had been working on was *Whose Body?*. She found an agent, and it was published in 1923. By that time, she was already writing another book in a series featuring Lord Peter.

After Cournos' departure, Sayers, at age 30, became involved with William White. The son of a clergyman, he was one year older than she. Biographer Barbara Reynolds recently supplied some new information about White, some of it obtained from White's daughter. In 1912, he became a bank clerk, taking up motorcycling and flying in his spare time. During World War I, he saw service with the Royal Engineers. He married in 1914 and had a daughter the following year. After demobilization, he entered the then fast-developing motor trade. He was accustomed to moving from place to place, sometimes joined by his family, sometimes not. In 1922, he took a room with friends in a flat above Sayers' in London. This is how they became acquainted.

Sayers' letters to her parents show that a good relationship existed between her and them. Thinking that White was lonely, she invited him to spend Christmas, 1922, at the rectory. They rode there together on his motorcycle. (She later had her own.) It is unlikely that she would have introduced this man to her mother and father had she known that he was married. It appears that Sayers often fed White and loaned him money. They took in theaters, dances, and dinners. Bill told his wife about such outings, assuring her that the relationship was not sexual.

In the spring of 1923, Sayers knew that she was pregnant. It is possible that only then did she learn that White had a wife. After asking Beatrice, his wife, to London from Southbourne for their wedding anniversary, he told her that Sayers was going to have his baby. Beatrice agreed to help; Sayers promised not to see Bill again and to put the child into the care of foster parents.

Beatrice White kept her word and did not reveal the child's existence until after Dorothy died. She had Sayers come to Southbourne for the delivery. The attending physician was Beatrice's brother, who had not been informed that he was delivering the child of his brother-in-law. During the accouchement, Beatrice occupied Sayers' London flat, sending on letters to her and posting her letters from London. Four year later, Beatrice divorced her husband because of his affairs with other women. After much thought, Sayers decided to keep her pregnancy secret from her parents; correctly or incorrectly, she feared that the knowledge would be very painful to them.

The solution to her dilemma was in the hands of her cousin Ivy Shrimpton and Ivy's widowed mother, who was Dorothy's aunt. These women made their living by fostering children in their home in Cowley, near Oxford. (Adoption became legal in England only in 1926.) Familiar with the good care they gave their charges, Sayers decided to trust her infant to them, relying on Ivy's discretion.

At the end of November, she took eight weeks' leave from Benson's, claiming illness. As it happened, she had been putting on weight before she became pregnant. No one seemed to suspect that her increasing girth was due to anything but her appetite. (After her pregnancy she became quite obese and made little effort to reduce.)

On January 3, 1924, John Anthony White was born in Southbourne. Sayers stayed there for three weeks breast-feeding her son. On January 27, she wrote to Ivy to say that the terms proposed by the latter were satisfactory (three pounds a month—Sayers was then earning more than six pounds a week) and that she was arriving with the infant on January 30. Ivy was to let her know when further expenses arose. Ivy continued to care for John Anthony after the death of her mother.

Another man now came into Sayers' life. This one she married. Oswald Arthur Fleming, known as Mac because of his Scottish lineage, had served in both the Boer and Great Wars and was working as a crime and motor-racing reporter when Sayers met him. He was divorced and did not support his ex-wife and two daughters. He wrote well, was talented at painting and photography and liked to cook. Dorothy found him good company; she loved beer and pubs and was glad to have him accompany her. Her decision to marry him may have been influenced by the fact that John Anthony needed a father and that at 33, her chances of marriage in post-war England were decreasing. At any rate, Mac and Dorothy were married on April 13, 1926.

They moved into Sayers' flat. Mac soon met John Anthony, two-and-a-half years old and still in Ivy's care. He would be there for a long time to come, because the apartment was small and someone to care for him would be very expensive. His mother was known to him as "Cousin Dorothy" and her husband as "Cousin Mac." Sayers had every intention of seeing that he continued to have the best of care and, ultimately, a good education. She worked very hard at Benson's and equally hard at her writing. She was making a name for herself—the publication of *Clouds of Witness* (1926) assured fans that Lord Peter would appear in more novels. For some time, she had been collecting material to write a biography of Wilkie Collins; that was an on-going project that appealed to her scholarly background (but one that she never completed). Mac, too, was busy. The couple acquired a car. They appeared to be happy.

Around this time, Sayers cut her hair. Since her hair sometimes fell out in abnormally large amounts, prompting her to wear a silver wig, she thought that her bob would improve the situation.

Sayers' father died at 74 in 1928. He had lived to read her first four novels and the anthology she had recently edited. The latter consisted of detective, mystery, and horror short stories and had an excellent introduction written by the editor. According to Barbara Reynolds, the Reverend Henry Sayers inspired the character of the Reverend Theodore Venables depicted in *The Nine Tailors* (1934). Mrs. Sayers died 10 months after her husband's death.

As Sayers' literary output increased, Mac's health deteriorated. Whether this was related to his wartime shell shock and gassing is not clear. By the summer of 1928, he had lost his job and as a freelance writer he earned very little. He became ill-tempered and more and more dependent on alcohol. They were able to enlarge the flat, but John Anthony remained with Ivy, who had moved to the village of Wescott Barton.

After Helen Sayers' death, Dorothy and Mac took over the house in Witham, Essex, where Mrs. Sayers and her sister Mabel had been living. Mabel remained there with them. In 1931, Sayers left Benson's to devote herself full time to writing, which she did mainly in Witham. Sometimes she was writing two books at the same time. By 1939, there were 12 Lord Peter Wimsey novels and two collection of short stories. The number of letters that she wrote was prodigious. An enthusiastic member of the Detection Club, she held various offices.

John Anthony was adopted in 1935. He was permitted to call Dorothy "Mother," but he was led to assume that she was his adopted mother. Always mindful about his education, she paid his expenses at a preparatory school. Mac's mental and physical health slowly worsened, imposing greater financial burdens on his wife. However, she did not abandon him and did what she could for him until his death in 1950. After her death, it was found that she had been sending regular payments to Mac's ex-wife.

One of Sayers' Oxford friends, Muriel St. Clare Byrne, taught at the Royal Academy of Dramatic Art. She persuaded Sayers to write a Wimsey play, promising her guidance. Dorothy loved theater, but had had no experience in play writing. Together they produced a comedy, *Busman's Honeymoon.* It opened in December, 1935, and ran for nine months. The whole project proved a delight to Dorothy; she attended rehearsals and traveled with the company when there were out-of-town performances. It was the beginning of a new phase of her creative career.

*Busman's Honeymoon* (1937) and a collection of short stories, *In the Teeth of the Evidence* (1939), were the last publications that involved Lord

Peter. There was also an unfinished manuscript, *Thrones, Dominations*, that was completed later by Jill Paton Walsh and published in 1998.

Sayers would now concentrate on the theater. On request for a play for the Canterbury Festival, she wrote *The Zeal of Thy Hand.* This religious play was presented at Canterbury in 1937, and then at London's Westminster Theatre. Later on tour, it proved to be a financial disaster. By 1951, she had written six additional plays. Of these, the best known in *The Man Born to Be King.* It is a series of radio plays on the life of Christ, first broadcast December, 1941, to October, 1942. Requested by the British Broadcasting Corporation, the series was used by the children's hour.

More and more, Sayers' opinion was sought on religious drama and on tenets of the Christian faith. She was skilled as an essayist as well as as a dramatist. She became much in demand as a lecturer. In fact, the last 20 years of her life were devoted to religious and scholarly writing.

She had begun to read Dante's *Inferno* in an air-raid shelter in 1944. Her last important undertaking was its translation. She completed the first two volumes, *Hell* and *Purgatory*, but *Inferno* had to be finished by her scholarly friend, Barbara Reynolds. Published in Penguin Classics in 1963, the Sayers work was more popular than other translations.

In 1950, the University of Durham conferred an honorary degree on Sayers.

Dorothy L. Sayers died suddenly on December 17, 1957, at Witham. She was 54.

After preparatory school, John Anthony won a scholarship to Malvern College, a school for boys. In World War II, he served with the technical branch of the Royal Air Force. In 1945, he went to Balliol College, Oxford on a government grant that covered tuition and fees; his mother, generous as usual, supplied an allowance. He graduated with a first-class degree. By that time, he had dropped John from his name. He found employment in an investment management company in London.

After the war, he needed a passport, and that required a birth certificate. On obtaining this, he learned the name of his biological mother. He went along with her deception until she died. A short time before his own death at 60, he said to an interviewer, "She did the very best she could."

*Whose Body?* is dedicated to Muriel ("Jim") Jaeger, a friend of Sayer's from her Mutual Admiration Society at Somerville College. The dedication noted: "If it had not been for your brutal insistence, Lord Peter would never have staggered through to the end of this enquiry." Sayers continued for some years to give Wimsey his day.

The real-life persons who probably contributed to Wimsey's character were mentioned previously. While working on the play, *Busman's Honeymoon,* Sayers was on the lookout for an actor to play. Lord Peter. When back at Oxford, she saw Maurice Roy Ridley, then the chaplain of Balliol college. She wrote to Muriel that he was the perfect Wimsey—"height, voice, charm, smile, manner, outline of features, everything." She had forgotten, or she chose to deny, that in 1913, during her student days, she had heard the same man recite a poem. He made such an impression at that time, that she wrote to a friend about him. It appears from this, that whether Sayers realized it or not, there was a physical resemblance between Ridley and her famous creation.

The frontispiece of *Clouds of Witnesseses* (1926) presented the latter's coat of arms and accompanying credentials.

> **WIMSEY, Peter Death Bredon, D.S.O.;** ***born*** **1890,** ***2nd son*** **of Mortimer Gerald Bredon Wimsey, 15th Duke of Denver, and of Honoria Lucasta,** ***daughter of*** **Francis Delagardie of Bellingham Manor, Hants.**
>
> ***Educated:*** **Eton College and Balliol College, Oxford (1st class honours, Sch. of Mod. Hist. 1912); served with H. M. Forces 1914/18 (Major, Rifle Brigade).** ***Author of:*** **"Notes on the Collecting of Incunabula," "The Murderer's Vade-Mecum," etc.** ***Recreations:*** **Criminology; bibliophily; music; cricket.**
>
> ***Clubs:*** **Marlborough; Egotists'.** ***Residences:*** **110A Piccadilly, W.; Bredon Hall, Duke's Denver, Norfolk.**
>
> ***Arms:*** **Sable, 3 mice courant, argent; crest, a domestic cat couched as to spring, proper; motto: As my Whimsy takes me.**

No doubt Sayers reveled in preparing this pedigree.

As we can see, Lord Peter is a man of many interests—from the books, we learn that he plays Bach well; he had a knowledge of chemistry; he is at home in the advertising business; and he is even versed in bell-ringing.

Dorothy loved puzzles, so it is natural that the difficult subject of bell ringing interested her. *The Nine Tailors* refer to church bells, and much of the book with the same title deals with this difficult art. Sayers must have portrayed it well: the Campanological Society of Great Britain invited her to be their vice-president, and the reader of *The Oxford Companion to Music* is referred to *The Nine Tailors* for a lucid explanation of change ringing.

Lord Peter had a talented gentleman's gentleman named Bunter, who added to the general interest.

Wimsey's future wife, Harriet Vane, was introduced in *Strong Poison* (1930). A writer of detective stories, she is not unlike Sayers. Lord Peter and Harriet married in *Busman's Honeymoon* (1937). (Sayers once declared that a detective married was a detective marred.) Subsequent publications mentioned a family.

It is difficult to regard Lord Peter, who sometimes sported a monocle, as anything but an anachronism. It strains the imagination to believe that a modern police investigator would have great confidence in a man who "has a hobby of criminal investigation." P.D. James has pointed out that those who are irritated by Dorothy Sayers frequently focus their dislike on her aristocratic detective.

If Peter seems antiquated, some of the ideas expressed by other characters are in tune with feminist thinking. To exemplify, Harriet Vane (1936) recites "a list of promising scholars, distinguished in their studies and subsequently extinguished by matrimony." Another fictional character (1934) declares that she doesn't want to be given money—her favorite teacher "doesn't think anything of a woman who can't be independent."

But P.D. James has also noted: "Like all good writers she created an unique and instantly recognizable world into which we can all escape for our comfort...." Thanks to Sayers' literary skill, Lord Peter Wimsey continues to charm readers. The books remain in print, and after Dorothy's death, television adaptations of them entertained ethusiastic audiences.

## *Listing of Works by Dorothy L. Sayers*

Dorothy Sayers Fleming did not use a pseudonym

---

### Lord Peter Wimsey Series

*Whose Body?* .......... 1923
*Clouds of Witnesses* .......... 1926

*Unnatural Death* . . . . . . . . . . . . . . . . . . . . . . . . . . . . . . . . . . . . . . . . . . .1927
(published in the U.S. as *The Dawson Pedigree*)
*The Unpleasantness at the Bellona Club* . . . . . . . . . . . . . . . . . . . . . . . . . . .1928
*Strong Poison* . . . . . . . . . . . . . . . . . . . . . . . . . . . . . . . . . . . . . . . . . . . . .1930
*Five Red Herrings* . . . . . . . . . . . . . . . . . . . . . . . . . . . . . . . . . . . . . . . . . .1931
(published in the U.S. as *Suspicious Characters*)
*Have His Carcase* . . . . . . . . . . . . . . . . . . . . . . . . . . . . . . . . . . . . . . . . . .1932
*Murder Must Advertise* . . . . . . . . . . . . . . . . . . . . . . . . . . . . . . . . . . . . . .1933
*The Nine Tailors* . . . . . . . . . . . . . . . . . . . . . . . . . . . . . . . . . . . . . . . . . .1934
*Gaudy Night* . . . . . . . . . . . . . . . . . . . . . . . . . . . . . . . . . . . . . . . . . . . . .1935
*Busman's Honeymoon* . . . . . . . . . . . . . . . . . . . . . . . . . . . . . . . . . . . . . . .1937
*In the Teeth of the Evidence* . . . . . . . . . . . . . . . . . . . . . . . . . . . . . . . . . .1939

## Other Crime Novels

(With Robert Ustace) *The Documents in the Case* . . . . . . . . . . . . . . . . . . .1930
(With members of The Detection Cub) *The Floating Admiral* . . . . . . . . .1931
(With members of The Detection Club) *Ask a Policeman* . . . . . . . . . . . . .1933
(With members of The Detection Club) *Six Against Scotland Yard* . . . . .1936
(published in England as *Six Against the Yard*)
*Busman's Honeymoon: A Love Story with Detective Interruptions* . . . . . . . . .1937
(adapted from previous works)
(With members of The Detection Club) *Double Death* . . . . . . . . . . . . . .1939
(With others) *The Scoop* and *Behind the Screen* . . . . . . . . . . . . . . . . . . . . .1983
(With Jill Paton Walsh) *Thrones, Dominations* . . . . . . . . . . . . . . . . . . . . .1998

## Short Story Collections

*Lord Peter Views the Body* . . . . . . . . . . . . . . . . . . . . . . . . . . . . . . . . . . . .1929
*In the Teeth of Evidence, and Other Stories* . . . . . . . . . . . . . . . . . . . . . . . .1940
*Hangman's Holiday* (abridged edition) . . . . . . . . . . . . . . . . . . . . . . . . . . .1942
*Even the Parrot: Exemplary Conversations for Enlightened Children* . . . . . .1944
*Lord Peter: A Collection of all the Lord Peter Wimsey Stories, 2nd ed.* . . . . . .1972

(Also numerous contributions to anthologies)

## Plays

(With Basil Mason) *The Silent Passenger* . . . . . . . . . . . . . . . . . . . . . . . . . .1935
(Phoenix Films screenplay adapted from a Sayers unpublished short story)
(With Muriel St. Clare Byrne) *Busman's Honeymoon: A Detective Comedy in Three Acts* . . . . . . . . . . . . . . . . . . . . . . . . . . . . . . . . . . . . . . . . . . . . .1937
*He That Should Come: A Nativity Play in One Act* (radio play) . . . . . . . . . .1939
*The Man Born to Be King: A Play-Cycle on the Life of Our Lord and Savior Jesus Christ* (12-episode radio series) . . . . . . . . . . . . . . . . . . . . . . . . . .1943
*Four Sacred Plays (The Zeal of Thy House, The Devil to Pay, He That Should Come, The Just Vengeance)* . . . . . . . . . . . . . . . . . . . . . . . . . . . . .1948

*The Emperor Constantine: A Chronicle* . . . . . . . . . . . . . . . . . . . . . . . . . .1951
*Love All* (play produced in 1940) . . . . . . . . . . . . . . . . . . . . . . . . . . . . .1984

## Translations

*Tristan in Brittany* by Thomas the Troubadour . . . . . . . . . . . . . . . . . . . .1929
*The Heart of Stone* by Dante . . . . . . . . . . . . . . . . . . . . . . . . . . . . . . . . .1946
(With Barbara Reynolds) *The Comedy of Dante Alighieri* (3 vols.) . .1949–1962
*The Song of Roland* . . . . . . . . . . . . . . . . . . . . . . . . . . . . . . . . . . . . . . .1957

## Essays

*The Greatest Drama Ever Staged* (Includes "The Greatest Drama Ever Staged" and "The Triumph of Easter") . . . . . . . . . . . . . . . . . . . . . . . .1939
*Strong Meat* . . . . . . . . . . . . . . . . . . . . . . . . . . . . . . . . . . . . . . . . . . . .1939
*Begin Here: A War-Time Essay* (published in the U. S. as *Begin Here: A Statement of Faith*) . . . . . . . . . .1940
*Creed or Chaos? and Other Essays in Popular Theology* . . . . . . . . . . . . . . .1941
*Unpopular Opinions* . . . . . . . . . . . . . . . . . . . . . . . . . . . . . . . . . . . . . . .1946
(With others) *The Great Mystery of Life Hereafter* . . . . . . . . . . . . . . . . .1957
*The Poetry of Search and the Poetry of Statement, and Other Posthumous Essays on Literature, Religion, and Language* . . . . . . . . . . . . . . . . . . . .1963
*Christian Letters to a Post-Christian World: A Selection of Essays*, edited by Roderick Jellema (also published as *The Whimsical Christian: Eighteen Essays*) . . . . . . . . . . . . . . . . . . . . . . . . . . . . . . . . . . . . .1969
*Are Women Human?* . . . . . . . . . . . . . . . . . . . . . . . . . . . . . . . . . . . . . . .1971
*A Matter of Eternity: Selections from the Writings of Dorothy L. Sayers*, edited by Rosamond Kent Sprague . . . . . . . . . . . . . . . . . . . . . . . . . . .1973

## Poetry

*Opus 1* . . . . . . . . . . . . . . . . . . . . . . . . . . . . . . . . . . . . . . . . . . . . . . .1916
(Contributor and editor with Wilfred Childe and Earp) *Oxford Poetry* .1917
*Catholic Tales and Christian Songs* . . . . . . . . . . . . . . . . . . . . . . . . . . . .1918
(Contributor and editor with Earp and E.F.A. Geach) *Oxford Poetry* . .1918
(Contributor and editor with Earp and Siegfried Sassoon) *Oxford Poetry* .1919
*Lord, I Thank Thee* . . . . . . . . . . . . . . . . . . . . . . . . . . . . . . . . . . . . . . . .1943
*The Story of Adam and Christ* . . . . . . . . . . . . . . . . . . . . . . . . . . . . . . . .1955

# 4

# Elizabeth MacKintosh *(Josephine Tey)*

Elizabeth MacKintosh in 1947 began to use the name Josephine Tey as what she termed an alias. This was the name of her great-grandmother from Suffolk. Her first pseudonym was Gordon Daviot, and she requested that she be listed in *Who's Who* under that name. She continued to use her own name privately. Professionally, she used both names, Tey for mysteries with the exception of her first. Today MacKintosh is best known as Josephine Tey.

The oldest of three daughters of Colin and Josephine (Horne) MacKintosh, Elizabeth was born in Inverness, Scotland in 1897. Colin was a greengrocer, and Josephine had been a teacher before she married. After studying at the Royal Academy located in her birthplace, Beth (as Elizabeth was known, started a course at Anstey Physical Training College in Birmingham, England, in 1914. She experienced Zeppelin raids and blackouts there, and, during vacations at home, worked in a nursing facility as part of the Volunteer Aid Detachment. She once made the statement that she never regretted studying physical culture rather than entering a university. For about eight years she earned her living in various parts of England as a physical training instructor.

In 1923, she returned to Scotland to nurse her mother, who had cancer. After the latter's death, she remained at home to keep house for her father until he died in 1950. Her two sisters married. She apparently had few friends; her obituary stated that she took little or no interest in the life of Inverness. She was known to enjoy reading, the movies and horse racing. Abandoning her first profession, she, like Agatha Christie and

Dorothy L. Sayers, was drawn to writing. She began her new career with the publication of poems and short pieces. *The Man in the Queue,* published in London in 1929, was her first mystery novel. She is reputed to have written it in less than three weeks, winning a competition for mystery thrillers sponsored by the publisher Methuen. With the author listed as Gordon Daviot, *Queue* introduced Alan Grant of Scotland Yard. Daviot is a village near Inverness and the MacKintosh family spent holidays there.

MacKintosh's first play, *Richard of Bordeaux,* was produced in 1932 and also used the Daviot pseudonym. The following year *Bordeaux* appeared as a book. The play ran for 14 months, produced and starred in by the distinguished actor John Gielgud. He noted later (as Sir John), "It was to the brilliant inspiration and sympathy of Gordon Daviot that I owed the biggest personal success of my career." Earlier he described MacKintosh as a strange character, proud and obstinate. He believed that she took more pride in her non-detective works than in her mysteries; he also thought that she bemoaned an inability to write original plots. (She did frequently depend on historical sources. For example, *The Franchise Affair* has a contemporary setting but is based on events that occurred in the 18th century.)

Tey is now remembered chiefly for her detective novels. Her second Inspector Grant mystery, *A Shilling for Candles* (1936), was the basis of an Alfred Hitchcock movie, *Young and Innocent,* made the following year. In her day, however, she was a popular dramatist also. In addition, she wrote three non-detective novels and a biography of Graham of Claverhouse, who led the Scottish rebellion against William of Orange. Heising has noted that MacKintosh is often called "the mystery writer for people who hate mysteries." This is because of her fondness for focusing on character rather than the hunt for the guilty.

MacKintosh shunned publicity, even refusing to give press interviews when she was a recognized author. Because so little is known about her background, critics are tempted to interpret much of her writing as autobiographical.This seems reasonable for *Miss Pym Disposes* (1947), which involves a murder in a physical education college for women, probably reflecting some of MacKintosh's experience at Birmingham. Incidentally, the fictional Miss Lucy Pym had a slight resemblance to Miss Marple, but Miss Pym did not appear in any subsequent Tey books.

During the last year of her life, MacKintosh knew that she had a fatal illness. She suffered alone, not wishing to see friends. She died in London on February 13, 1952, at age 55. Among her effects was the manuscript to *The Singing Sands,* apparently only just completed. She willed the proceeds from her writing to the National Trust for Places of Historic Interest or Natural Beauty. This has provided a considerable sum over the years.

Inspector Alan Grant played an important role in five of Tey's books and had a minor role in one. Although employed by Scotland Yard, Grant was a "gentleman cop," independently wealthy thanks to an aunt who left him her money. Since he was a bachelor, a Mrs. Tinker "does for him." (When the reader first meets him, his landlady feeds him.) He had a taste for fine foods, but often ate out. He enjoyed fishing, especially in Scotland. A sensitive individual, he had a "passion for faces" and believed he could deduce an individual's character from facial appearance. He was very conscientious, giving much thought to whatever professional situation presented itself, and was likely to talk over the facts of a case with Sergeant Williams. "There isn't a murder type," he contended, "People murder for many different reasons." All of the books in which Grant played a prominent part are popular. *The Daughter of Time* was highly regarded by Howard Haycraft.

When the book opens, Grant was in the hospital, incapacitated by a fall through a trapdoor when he was in pursuit of a criminal. His friend, the actress Marta Hallard, brought him some photos of originals of historic figures in the National Portrait Gallery.

Grant became interested in the face of Richard III (King of England 1483–85). Most people educated in England think they know something about this monarch, although the knowledge may or may not be accurate: he was a hunchback, he murdered his nephews in the Tower of London to assure his succession to the throne, and he was killed while looking for a horse to enable his escape from his enemies. These facts are reinforced by Shakespeare's *Richard III.* Grant did not see evil in the face he studied, and experience had given him confidence in his judgment. He decided to investigate the matter as thoroughly as possible.

The nurses caring for him provided him with school books that recounted the familiar version of Richard's life. Sergeant Williams found more books. Marta helped by producing Brent Carradine, a young American who had time to locate materials in the British Museum. Using historical records as a background and employing his logic for solving contemporary murders, Grant discarded hearsay evidence and reached a plausible theory as to who benefited by discrediting the King. He came to the conclusion that Richard was innocent of the murder of his nephews, the real culprit being Henry VII, successor to Edward.

Tey used the word "tonypandy" to refer to such alteration of facts. She noted that the term refers to an incident that took place in

**Richard III by an unknown artist. The face that inspired *The Daughter of Time*. By courtesy of the National Portrait Gallery, London.**

Tonypandy, Wales, in 1910, and was reported inaccurately. The inaccuracies persisted because those who knew otherwise failed to speak up. The occurrence of tonypandy is the theme of *The Daughter of Time.* The title is from a proverb—"Time is the daughter of truth."

Historians disagree about the facts concerning Richard III, with contemporary viewpoints more inclined to favor innocence than the guilt claimed by earlier authorities. The important consideration is how Tey developed the story from Grant's viewpoint. That she did it skillfully is clear from the fact that after half a century, *The Daughter of Time* is still a favorite of detective story readers.

## *Listing of Works by Elizabeth MacKintosh*

PSEUDONYMS: Gordon Daviot, Josephine Tey

---

### INSPECTOR GRANT MYSTERIES

*The Man in the Queue* (as Gordon Daviot) . . . . . . . . . . . . . . . . . . . . . . . . .1929
(republished as *Killer in the Crowd*) (as Josephine Tey) . . . . . . . . . . . . .1954
*A Shilling for Candles* (as Josephine Tey) . . . . . . . . . . . . . . . . . . . . . . . . .1936
*The Franchise Affair* (as Josephine Tey ) . . . . . . . . . . . . . . . . . . . . . . . . . .1948
(Grant has a minor part)
*To Love and Be Wise* (as Josephine Tey) . . . . . . . . . . . . . . . . . . . . . . . . . .1950
*The Daughter of Time* (as Josephine Tey) . . . . . . . . . . . . . . . . . . . . . . . . .1951
*The Singing Sands* (as Josephine Tey) . . . . . . . . . . . . . . . . . . . . . . . . . . .1952

### OTHER WORKS

*Kif: An Unvarnished History* (as Gordon Daviot) . . . . . . . . . . . . . . . . . . . .1929
*The Expensive Halo* (as Gordon Daviot) . . . . . . . . . . . . . . . . . . . . . . . . . .1931
*Richard of Bordeaux* (as Gordon Daviot) . . . . . . . . . . . . . . . . . . . . . . . . . .1933
*The Laughing Woman* (as Gordon Daviot) . . . . . . . . . . . . . . . . . . . . . . . . .1934
*Queen of Scots* (as Gordon Daviot) . . . . . . . . . . . . . . . . . . . . . . . . . . . . . .1934
*Claverhouse* (as Gordon Daviot) . . . . . . . . . . . . . . . . . . . . . . . . . . . . . . . .1937
*The Stars Bow Down* (as Gordon Daviot) . . . . . . . . . . . . . . . . . . . . . . . . . .1939
*Leith Sands and Other Short Plays* (as Gordon Daviot) . . . . . . . . . . . . . . .1946
*Miss Pym Disposes* (as Josephine Tey) . . . . . . . . . . . . . . . . . . . . . . . . . . .1946
*Brat Farrar* (as Josephine Tey) . . . . . . . . . . . . . . . . . . . . . . . . . . . . . . . . .1949
(republished in the U.S. as *Come and Kill Me*) (as Josephine Tery) . . . .1951
*The Privateer* (as Gordon Daviot) . . . . . . . . . . . . . . . . . . . . . . . . . . . . . . .1952
Plays, 3 vols. (as Gordon Daviot) . . . . . . . . . . . . . . . . . . . . . . . . . . . . .1953–54

# 5

# Ngaio Marsh

A British newspaper once noted that although Ngaio Marsh was born in New Zealand, "we are entitled to consider her as one of us." England may claim her, but she spent the first 33 years of her life on New Zealand soil. If she is not strictly a British detective story writer, she is considered an author of that genre's Golden Age. For this reason we present her here in her special category of an Anglo–New Zealander mystery writer.

(Edith) Ngaio Marsh was the only child of Henry Edward and Rose Elizabeth (Seager) Marsh. Ngaio is pronounced "ny-o" and is a Maori word for a flowering tree found in New Zealand. She was born in Christchurch, April 23, 1895, not 1899, as she often claimed. An emigrant from England, her father was a clerk in the Bank of New Zealand. Her mother was born in New Zealand, her maternal grandfather having served as a policeman and later as supervisor of a new mental asylum near Christchurch. The parents provided a loving environment for Ngaio; she remembered being read to at an early age; there was a cat named Susie and a spaniel named Tip. Henry was thrifty, a man of high principles and blessed with a sense of humor; he was also antireligious and versed in natural science. Rose was understanding, conventional and a talented amateur actress. To her daughter, it seemed that the responsibility of her upbringing was in her mother's hands. Both parents were readers.

Ngaio's autobiography entitled *Black Beech and Honeydew* and published in 1965 had some descriptions of the land of her birth and of the country's culture. The title refers to a piece of friable leaf-dust found between the pages of a photograph album. By way of explanation, honeydew is a saccharine deposit found on many plant leaves. In Ngaio's own words: "It might have fallen from a native beech tree, clothed in black

Ngaio Marsh about 1951 by Pearl Freeman. By courtesy of Alexander Turnbull Library, Wellington, NZ.

moss; a tree that on a warm morning fifty years ago in the foothills of New Zealand, sweated little globules of honeydew."

A select dame school, home schooling by her mother and then a governess were part of Ngaio's early education. At 15 she entered St. Margaret's College, a private school run by the Church of England. (She remained a high-church Anglican.) Here she learned how to improve her writing and developed an abiding passion for the plays and sonnets of Shakespeare, her favorite remaining *Hamlet.* During this period, she became interested in amateur theatricals. According to her autobiography, it was the ambience of backstage that she found immensely satisfying; the forming and growth of a play and its precipitation into its final shape. Eventually she knew that she preferred to direct rather than act. She was also studying art. She wrote a children's play and some children's stories, illustrating the latter herself.

From 1915 to 1920, Ngaio attended Canterbury University College of Art, which offered painting holidays. She paid her way by teaching individual children. Painting would always be an important part of Ngaio's life, but she seemed to realize that she would never become, according to the tastes of the day, a good artist.

Her native country was at war most of this period, creating a dearth of young men between 18 and 40. Those who had survived Gallipoli, the Middle East, and Passchendaele were not granted leave to come home. Ned Bristed, a dear friend since childhood and with whom she was corresponding when he was fighting in Europe, became a casualty of the war.

After art college, Ngaio turned to a new career, one that would become a dominant part of her life—the stage. At first she became an actress with the Allan Wilkie Shakespeare Company, touring New Zealand for two years. Then she joined another professional company formed by Rosemary Rees. This soon failed, and Ngaio returned to Christchurch. Here she involved herself in charity shows as actress, producer and director. She also wrote for local newspapers. In addition to her journalistic efforts, she wrote plays and poems and began a novel about New Zealand.

Through amateur theatricals she became friendly with an English upper-class family named Rhodes, who had come from Britain to live on a sheep farm. The friendship was a lasting one, and after the Rhodeses returned to England, they invited her to visit them. (Fictional characters named Lamprey that appeared in several Marsh books were based on Rhodes family members.)

In 1928, Ngaio set sail for England via the Cape of Good Hope. The vessel's travel time was scheduled to take ten weeks.To provide her with a source of income she had contracted with New Zealand newspapers to write travel articles. The Rhodeses entertained her royally, introducing her to high society and even inviting her on trips to Monte Carlo and other places. The young New Zealander remained in England until 1932. She worked as an interior decorator and with Nellie Rhodes in operating a gift shop that soon failed. As might be expected, she took in as many as possible London stage performances.

Marsh's career as a writer of detective stories began in England when she created Roderick Alleyn. Dulwich College, where her father had studied, was founded by an Elizabethan actor named Edward Alleyn. So, "as a sort of compliment to Popsey," she named her detective Alleyn. Introduced in *A Man Lay Dying*, he would bring her fame and fortune.

Rose Marsh was able to visit Ngaio in England, however, by 1932, she was dying, and her daughter came home to care for her mother. The manuscript about Alleyn was left with an agent.

It was published in 1934, and there was a contract for future books. Her permanent residence for the next 16 years was New Zealand. She and her father lived in Marton Cottage that he had built for his family many years previously. In 1937, the now-established writer paid a long visit to England to gather material for her stories.

World War II at first posed little danger of an invasion of New Zealand. With the fall of Singapore, there was a real threat. Marsh did her bit; she was a Red Cross ambulance driver whose job was to transport wounded servicemen from ports to hospitals.

Despite the pressure of having to produce detective novels as a means of support, Marsh began an activity that would occupy her for the next 30 years—producing Shakespearean plays. She used students and experienced amateurs, always setting high standards and instilling enthusiasm; suitable music was often commissioned. In 1948, her dedication was recognized by an award from the Order of the British Empire (O.B.E.) for services to literature and theater in New Zealand.

After her father died in 1948, Marsh followed a pattern of devoting about nine months of the year to writing and the remaining three to production and direction of plays by Shakespeare. She stated that had she not directed 10 plays by the immortal bard, she would have written 10 more detective stories. Judging from her autobiography, the former was her great interest. Also, she apparently did not regard the mystery as great literature, once writing, "I suppose the one thing that can always be said in favor of the genre is that inside the convention the author may write with as good a style as he or she can command."

The University of Canterbury in 1963 conferred the degree of Doctor of Literature. Three years later, Marsh became Dame Commander of the British Empire, largely because of her effort of behalf of the theater (she referred to the honor as her "damery"). It was a great satisfaction to her that some of her students became known outside New Zealand in the fields of stage and film. She kept in touch with many who had worked on her productions.

While the public in New Zealand associated Marsh with theater, the British public knew her as a popular writer of detective stories. In 1959, *Scales of Justice* received the Red Herring Award from the British Crime Writers Association. Marsh's books were well known in the United States, and in 1960 she visited both Japan and this country as part of a long voyage to England. Because of an aversion to air travel, she took a train from San Francisco to New York.

Friends and relatives have supplied bits and pieces of information about Marsh's personality. John Dacres-Manning, her cousin and chief inheritor, contended that she disliked writing, but that it provided her a comfortable life style and helped to pay for the theater work with which she was associated. He noted her magnetic personality and a rapport with children equaled by few; he remembered personages she had entertained such as Lawrence Olivier, Vivien Leigh and Anthony Quayle. She impressed crime writer Julian Symons with her charm. One of her agents, Edmund Cork (who represented Agatha Christie), thought of Marsh as a humble person. Biographer Margaret Lewis—who did not know Marsh—wrote that when her subject was affluent she rented a flat in a fashionable part of London, wore expensive and stylish clothes to suit her 5-foot-10-inch frame and striking appearance, walked a Siamese cat on a jeweled lead and drove a costly Jaguar. (Another Jaguar sports car was shipped back to New Zealand, to become the most famous vehicle on South Island.) Marton Cottage was transformed into a southern hemisphere replica of an English country house with appropriate garden and a mural of *The Tempest* painted over the drawing room fireplace. Despite all that, Marsh was, according to Lewis, a very shy person.

Marsh's last trip to the United Kingdom was in 1974. She missed the previous glamor of passenger ships—air travel had changed that. During her stay in England she had surgery for cancer. Added to that, she suffered from angina, poor eyesight and deafness, but she continued to write, and friends saw that she was taken to theatrical performances.

In 1978, the Mystery Writers of America made her a Grand Master and presented her with a much-sought-after Edgar.

Ngaio Marsh died on February 18, 1982, in Christchurch.

Her chief legacy was 32 mystery novels, of which one of her favorites was *Colour Scheme.* Nine took place in English country houses while seven were set in New Zealand. About half had some type of theatrical background, even presenting murder onstage. Many of the novels reflected her training in painting—*Clutch of Constables* with its double-entendre title refers not only to the police, but also to a British painter. Four novels were adapted for television in New Zealand. A great legacy. And in the year 2000, all 32 mystery novels are in print.

Marsh made a point of beginning with people, rather than plot. First on the list of people was Roderick Alleyn of Scotland Yard, her chief investigator. Alleyn belonged to the nobility, but was a second son. Educated at Oxford, he was a student of Shakespeare. He had once worked in the Foreign Office, but left for reasons undivulged. He then became a professional policeman, rising through the ranks from constable to chief superintendent. His associates were Nigel Bathgate, a journalist; Inspector Edward Fox, known to Alleyn as "Br'er Fox" or "Foxkins"; Sergeant Bailey, photographer; and Sergeant Thompson, fingerprint expert. Alleyn was tall and lean with blue eyes and dark hair. A likable man, he did not drink on duty, opposed capital punishment, distrusted conjecture and did not attribute much importance to motive. He did stress opportunity. Many of the books in the series recounted his methodical investigation of all persons closely or remotely connected with a murder. Alleyn's age is not clear. In *Artists in Crisis,* published in 1938, he was 45. If he aged in proportion to publication date, he would have been 87 in *Photo Finish.* This was obviously not so, as we shall see, and in that book, Marsh makes no mention of her C.I.'s age.

Marsh involved her appealing creation in a variety of unique locales and situations such as thermal pools and Morris dancing. Her best known murder weapon was probably a pistol rigged to fire with the first use of the piano's soft pedal in a performance of Rachmaninoff's "Prelude in C Sharp Minor."

Alleyn was not a bachelor. Returning from New Zealand, on shipboard he met Agatha Troy, an established artist (and one with peculiiar habits—she once left a preliminary sketch of the prime minister on the floor, to have the cat ruin it by sitting on it). He fell in love with her, and eventually they married. He took her career seriously and was very proud of her accomplishment. The Alleyns became parents of Ricky, who was kidnapped in one book and appeared in another as an adult.

A brief look at *Photo Finish*, published in 1980, gives the reader a glance into a Marsh mystery.

Isabella Sommita, world famous opera star of Italian birth, was the subject of a series of unflattering and insulting photographs taken by someone who published them under the name Strix. The prima donna was furious at the unknown photographer; she also feared him and told a young protégé that she was in direct line to be murdered.

Montague V. Reece, Sommita's rich friend and patron, commissioned Troy to paint a portrait of the diva. He invited the artist and Alleyn to New Zealand as his guests while the sittings were in progress. He also hoped that Alleyn would be a protection against the objectionable photographer. Through Interpol Scotland Yard had received some rumors that Sommita in the past might have been involved in the international drug scene. Alleyn was given some facts about her and Reece and told to keep an eye open.

The Reece establishment was in Westland, on an island on Lake Waihoe. Marsh described the approach: "At this hour the Lake was perfectly unrufled and held the blazing magnet of an outrageous sunset. Fingers of land reached out bearing elegant trees that reversed themselves in the water. Framed by these and far beyond them was the Island and on the Island Mr. Reece's Lodge."

The singer was currently involved with a young man named Rupert Bartholomew who had written an opera for her. It was about to be performed at the time of the Alleyns' arrival, and important personages from the world of music were at the lodge for the event. Bartholomew had realized, too late, that his opera was worthless and would be an embarrassment to all. The diva was furious and refused to cancel. At the end of the performance, the composer clumsily announced what he knew to be the truth.

Later in the evening, Sommita was found dead in her bedroom, her heart pierced by a stiletto thrust through another uncomplimentary photograph.

A terrific wind storm swept the lake, cutting communication lines and making travel by boat impossible. Reece put Alleyn in charge of the investigation until New Zealand police could be called in.

There were crucial questions to be answered, among them: Should they be looking for a madman? Or was the murder a coldly calculated act? Was Strix still at the lodge and who was he? Was Bartholemew, whom many suspected, guilty? Why did the prima donna's maid, Maria, balk at giving her maiden name? What is the significance of the initials M.V.R.? What of the drug ring?

By the time the local police arrived, Alleyn was able to give them sufficient information to make two arrests.

## *Listing of Works by Ngaio Marsh*

Ngaio Marsh did not use a pseudonym

### Roderick Alleyn Series

*A Man Lay Dead* . . . . . . . . 1934
*Enter a Murderer* . . . . . . . . 1935
*The Nursing-Home Murder* (with Henry Jellett) . . . . . . . . 1935
*Death in Ecstasy* . . . . . . . . 1936
*Vintage Murder* . . . . . . . . 1937
*Artists in Crime* . . . . . . . . 1938
*Death in a White Tie* . . . . . . . . 1938
*Overture to Death* . . . . . . . . 1939
*Death at the Bar* . . . . . . . . 1940
*Death of a Peer* . . . . . . . . 1940
(published in England as *Surfeit of Lampreys*)
*Death and the Dancing Footman* . . . . . . . . 1941
*Colour Scheme* . . . . . . . . 1943
*Died in the Wool* . . . . . . . . 1945
*Final Curtain* . . . . . . . . 1947
*Swing, Brother, Swing* . . . . . . . . 1949
(published in the U.S. as *A Wreath for Rivera*)
*Opening Night* . . . . . . . . 1951
(published in the U.S. as *Night at the Vulcan*)
*Spinsters in Jeopardy* . . . . . . . . 1953
(published in the U.S. as *The Bride of Death*)
*Scales of Justice* . . . . . . . . 1955
*Death of a Fool* . . . . . . . . 1956
(published in England as *Off with His Head*)
*Singing in the Shrouds* . . . . . . . . 1958
*False Scent* . . . . . . . . 1960
*Hand in Glove* . . . . . . . . 1962
*Dead Water* . . . . . . . . 1963
*Killer Dolphin* . . . . . . . . 1966
(published in England as *Death at the Dolphin*)
*Clutch of Constables* . . . . . . . . 1968
*When in Rome* . . . . . . . . 1970
*Tied Up in Tinsel* . . . . . . . . 1972
*Black as He's Painted* . . . . . . . . 1974
*Last Ditch* . . . . . . . . 1977
*Grave Mistake* . . . . . . . . 1978
*Photo Finish* . . . . . . . . 1980
*Light Thickens* . . . . . . . . 1982

### AUTOBIOGRAPHY

*Black Beech and Honeydew* . . . . . . . . . . . . . . . . . . . . . . . . 1965 (rev. ed., 1981)

### NONFICTION

*New Zealand* (with Randal Matthew Burdon) . . . . . . . . . . . . . . . . . . . . . 1942

### JUVENILE PLAY

*The Christmas Tree* . . . . . . . . . . . . . . . . . . . . . . . . . . . . . . . . . . . . 1962

### JUVENILE

*New Zealand* . . . . . . . . . . . . . . . . . . . . . . . . . . . . . . . . . . . . . . . 1964

### SHORT FICTION

*The Collected Shorter Fiction of Ngaio Marsh,* ed. Douglas G. Greene (published in England as *Death on the Air and Other Stories*) . . . . . . . . . . . . . . . . . . . . 1989

(Author of plays, reviews, articles; contributor to anthologies)

# 6
# Gladys Mitchell

Gladys Mitchell wrote some 50 books before she permanently quit teaching school to devote herself full time to writing. Although *Publishers Weekly* termed her "one of England's most eminent writers of crime fiction," her books have not been as well known in the United States as in Britain. Some critics consider Mitchell, who enjoyed a long life, the last of the writers of the Golden Age.

Gladys Maude Winifred Mitchell was born April 19, 1901, in Cowley, near Oxford, England. Her parents were James and Anne Julia Maude (Simmons) Mitchell. Her father was of Scottish descent, her mother English. Because James had been forced to enter the work force at age 13, he was determined that his daughters would be properly educated.

The family made several moves when Gladys was a youngster. While attending a village school, she decided to be a teacher. At age 10, as a student at the Green School, Isleworth, Middlesex, she won third prize in a short-story competition aimed at girls of 15. After graduation from the Green School in 1918, she entered Goldsmith's College, London University, obtaining a Board of Education Teacher's Certificate in 1921. While teaching, she studied as an extramural student at University College, London, and received an extramural diploma in English and European history in 1926.

Mitchell taught English and history at St. Paul's School, Brentford, Middlesex from 1921 to 1925. For the next 14 years she was employed by St. Ann's Senior Girls' School in Ealing. During this time, she coached a hopeful hurdles champion. She had no position for two years because of illness. Employed at Brentford Senior Girls' School from 1941 to 1950, she taught Spanish and history as well as involving herself in physical education. After another hiatus in her teaching career, she became a member of the staff of the Matthew Arnold Secondary Country School for Girls, Staines, Middlesex, as a teacher of history and English. She also wrote plays for student performance. Her final retirement from teaching came in 1961.

Described as having blue eyes and fair hair and weighing about 130 pounds, Mitchell listed her avocational interests as athletics, swimming and architecture, the latter from Roman to 18th century English. Her favorite authors were Louisa May Alcott, Ivy Compton-Burnett and P.G. Wodehouse. She also read the Elizabethan poets and the Border ballads and admired the writings of Ngaio Marsh. Mitchell kept up on real-life murders and read reminiscences of the great lawyers. In addition, she studied Freud.

She enjoyed travel, which was possible during school vacations. She visited, among other places, all the Mediterranean countries except Egypt, and was familiar with most Western European countries as well as Madeira and the Canary Islands.

Her first four novels were rejected; her first book was published in 1929, and her last in 1984. A glance at her credits will show her prodigious output—more amazing still because for more than half of her writing career, she simultaneously held teaching positions. The mystery novels for adults were written under her own name, as were nine books for young people. Mitchell also produced non-mystery novels using the pseudonym Stephen Hockaby. According to her, she considered them rather good; she abandoned them because the rewards were so utterly inadequate in the light of the research expended on them. (Mitchell once stated, "...my books have never made much money.") As Malcolm Torrie she wrote a six-book series that introduced a sleuth named Timothy Herring who was interested in the preservation of historical buildings.

She found each book difficult to write, partly because, even if she had a plan, she seldom stuck to it. Since she wrote in longhand, the manuscript was sent out for typing. This was because she disliked the noise of the typewriter; also, because she claimed that she could not spell on the machine, she was prone to alter the typescript, which meant additional typing.

Mitchell held memberships in the Detection Club, the Crime Writers' Club and the Society of Authors; she was also a fellow of the Ancient Monuments Society. In 1976, she won a Silver Dagger Award. She listed herself as Conservative in politics and with regard to religion, agnostic. (A much younger sister was a Dominican nun, although the Mitchells were not Roman Catholic.) At 75, Mitchell claimed that with a rifle she could hit a post card 10 times out of 10 at 25 paces.

Late in life she was asked whether she was an optimist and whether the writing of crime novels was in any way therapeutic for her. Here is her answer:

> Yes, I suppose I am an optimist, I would far rather ignore (from cowardice, I think) the seamy side of life. I have only academic knowledge of romance and sex, love to laugh, and hate and detest violence and cruelty. The writing of crime novels is in no way therapeutic to me. I am fascinated by murder because it is about the last thing I would think of committing, apart from blackmail.

She lived in Dorset during the latter part of her writing career. She died July 27, 1983, at 82.

Gladys Mitchell's greatest claim to fame is her creation of Mrs. Beatrice Adela Lestrange Bradley. Dame Beatrice, as she became in 1955, was the central character in 66 detective mysteries. Her physical characteristics, as described, were not attractive: an elderly beaky-mouthed female who cackled, whose skin color was yellow, whose hands were referred to as claws; she was like a pterodactyl. Even her taste in clothes was suspect—she was seen in an outfit of "sage green, purple and yellow." There were some redeeming features—for example, she had raven hair without "a touch of grey"; she was quick-eyed; and she had a beautiful voice. Professionally, she was trained in medicine—she had a clinic and was consulting psychiatrist to the Home Office. Dame Beatrice was respected by the police and had an air of confidence about her. She was a widow living in comfortable circumstances at the Stone House in the village of Wandles Parva in Hampshire. She maintained a town house in Kensington.These residences, however, did not prevent her taking off for Italy or elsewhere if she were needed.

At one point, George, her chauffeur, was driving a Jaguar; she had a French cook named Henri. Henri's wife, Celestine, was Dame Beatrice's housekeeper/lady's maid. At first her Watson was a curate. Later that role was played by her secretary Laura, who eventually married Chief Detective-Inspector Robert Gavin of the C.I.D. Dame Beatrice's son from her first marriage, Ferdinand Lestrange, was a lawyer. A son by another marriage went to India to specialize in tropical diseases. Assorted relatives were introduced. These people and others often called in Dame Beatrice for advice when perplexing problems arose. This unusual woman not only solved every crime presented to her, but had innumerable other abilities; she was versed in "a thirties form of karate" as well as in lip reading; she could fix a bathroom ball cock; she could substitute for a concert cellist—and so on. This lady who held a number of degrees, earned and honorary, sometimes had advanced views—she favored birth control in the 1930s, had extramarital love affairs, and had even committed what she considered justifiable killing.

Mitchell made it clear that Dame Beatrice's appearance was based on two delightful and intelligent women she knew in her youth; the lady's mannerisms, costume, and formidable brain were entirely the author's invention. In 1929, Dame Beatrice was intended to be about 55. This meant that for her, the passage of time had to be ignored. In contrast, Laura's life progressed naturally with each new book of the series.

The settings and characters were diverse—for example, the locale of *St. Peter's Finger* was a convent on the moors, and word association and nudism were the subjects of *Printer's Error. Say It with Flowers* portrayed dilettante diggers for Romano-British specimens; *The Death Cap Dancers* focused on a folk-dance group staying at a Youth Hostel in Yorkshire and touched on transvestitism. About her settings, Mitchell stated, "My vocational interests are governed by British Ordnance Survey maps, as a definite real setting is usually necessary to the formation of my plots."

Along with psychology, supernatural phenomena are commonly dealt with in the Dame Beatrice series—to illustrate, the Loch Ness monster comes into *Winking at the Brim*. It is the opinion of critic Michelle Slung that Mitchell's lifelong fascination with the antiquities of the British Isles and their accompanying superstitions was mirrored in her writing.

Some critics have not been kind to Gladys Mitchell, but apart from this, the *Times Literary Supplement*, made the following appraisal of her output: "...the overwhelmingly positive response her work has received from generations of readers is probably the clearest testimony to its strengths and quality as detective fiction."

## *Listing of Works by Gladys Mitchell*

PSEUDONYMS: Stephen Hockaby, Malcolm Torrie

### BEATRICE LESTRANGE BRADLEY SERIES

*Speedy Death* .......................................... 1929
*The Mystery of a Butcher's Shop* .......................................... 1929
*The Longer Bodies* .......................................... 1930
*The Saltmarsh Murders* .......................................... 1932
*Death at the Opera* .......................................... 1934
(published in the U.S. as *Death in the Wet*)
*The Devil at Saxon Wall* .......................................... 1935

*Dead Men's Morris* .......... 1936
*Come Away, Death* .......... 1937
*St. Peter's Finger* .......... 1938
*Printer's Error* .......... 1939
*Brazen Tongue* .......... 1940
*Hangman's Curfew* .......... 1941
*When Last I Died* .......... 1941
*Laurels are Poison* .......... 1942
*The Worsted Viper* .......... 1943
*Sunset Over Soho* .......... 1943
*My Father Sleeps* .......... 1944
*The Rising of the Moon* .......... 1945
*Here Comes a Chopper* .......... 1946
*Death and the Maiden* .......... 1947
*The Dancing Druids* .......... 1948
*Tom Brown's Body* .......... 1949
*Groaning Spinney* .......... 1950
*The Devil's Elbow* .......... 1951
*The Echoing Strangers* .......... 1952
*Merlin's Furlong* .......... 1953
*Faintly Speaking* .......... 1954
*Watson's Choice* .......... 1955
*Twelve Horses and the Hangman's Noose* .......... 1956
*The Twenty-Third Man* .......... 1957
*Spotted Hemlock* .......... 1958
*The Man Who Grew Tomatoes* .......... 1959
*Say It with Flowers* .......... 1960
*Nodding Canaries* .......... 1961
*My Bones Will Keep* .......... 1962
*Adders on the Heath* .......... 1963
*Death of a Delft Blue* .......... 1964
*Pageant of Murder* .......... 1965
*The Croaking Raven* .......... 1966
*Skeleton Island* .......... 1967
*Three Quick and Five Dead* .......... 1968
*Dance to Your Daddy* .......... 1969
*Gory Dew* .......... 1970
*Lament for Leto* .......... 1971
*A Hearse on May-Day* .......... 1972
*The Murder of Busy Lizzie* .......... 1973
*A Javelin for Jonah* .......... 1974
*Winking at the Brim* .......... 1974
*Convent on Styx* .......... 1975
*The Croaking Raven* .......... 1975
*Late, Late in the Evening* .......... 1976
*Fault in the Structure* .......... 1977

*Noonday and Night* . . . . . . . . . . . . . . . . . . . . . . . . . . . . . .1977
*Mingled with Venom* . . . . . . . . . . . . . . . . . . . . . . . . . . . . . .1978
*Wraiths and Changelings* . . . . . . . . . . . . . . . . . . . . . . . . . . .1978
*The Mudflats of the Dead* . . . . . . . . . . . . . . . . . . . . . . . . . . .1979
*Nest of Vipers* . . . . . . . . . . . . . . . . . . . . . . . . . . . . . . . .1979
*Uncoffined Clay* . . . . . . . . . . . . . . . . . . . . . . . . . . . . . . .1980
*The Whispering Knights* . . . . . . . . . . . . . . . . . . . . . . . . . . .1980
*The Death-Cap Dancers* . . . . . . . . . . . . . . . . . . . . . . . . . . . .1981
*Lovers, Make Moan* . . . . . . . . . . . . . . . . . . . . . . . . . . . . . .1981
*Death of a Burrowing Mole* . . . . . . . . . . . . . . . . . . . . . . . . . .1982
*Here Lies Gloria Mundy* . . . . . . . . . . . . . . . . . . . . . . . . . . .1982
*Cold, Lone and Still* . . . . . . . . . . . . . . . . . . . . . . . . . . . . .1983
*The Greenstone Griffins* . . . . . . . . . . . . . . . . . . . . . . . . . . .1983
(With others) *Crime on the Coast* and *No Flowers by Request* . . . . . . . . . . .1984
*The Crozier Pharaohs* . . . . . . . . . . . . . . . . . . . . . . . . . . . . .1984
*No Winding-Sheet* . . . . . . . . . . . . . . . . . . . . . . . . . . . . . . .1984

## Timothy Herring Series (as Malcolm Torrie)

*Heavy as Lead* . . . . . . . . . . . . . . . . . . . . . . . . . . . . . . . .1966
*Late and Cold* . . . . . . . . . . . . . . . . . . . . . . . . . . . . . . . .1967
*Your Secret Friend* . . . . . . . . . . . . . . . . . . . . . . . . . . . . . .1968
*Churchyard Salad* . . . . . . . . . . . . . . . . . . . . . . . . . . . . . . .1969
*Shades of Darkness* . . . . . . . . . . . . . . . . . . . . . . . . . . . . . .1970
*Bismarck Herring* . . . . . . . . . . . . . . . . . . . . . . . . . . . . . . .1971

## Novels (as Stephen Hockaby)

*Marsh Hay* . . . . . . . . . . . . . . . . . . . . . . . . . . . . . . . . . .1933
*Seven Stars and Orion* . . . . . . . . . . . . . . . . . . . . . . . . . . . .1934
*Gabriel's Hold* . . . . . . . . . . . . . . . . . . . . . . . . . . . . . . . .1935
*Shallow Brown* . . . . . . . . . . . . . . . . . . . . . . . . . . . . . . . .1936
*Grand Master* . . . . . . . . . . . . . . . . . . . . . . . . . . . . . . . . .1939

## Other (including children's books)

*Outlaws of the Border* . . . . . . . . . . . . . . . . . . . . . . . . . . . .1936
*The Three Fingerprints* . . . . . . . . . . . . . . . . . . . . . . . . . . . .1940
*Holiday River* . . . . . . . . . . . . . . . . . . . . . . . . . . . . . . . .1948
*The Seven Stones Mystery* . . . . . . . . . . . . . . . . . . . . . . . . . . .1949
*The Malory Secret* . . . . . . . . . . . . . . . . . . . . . . . . . . . . . .1950
*Pam at Storne Castle* . . . . . . . . . . . . . . . . . . . . . . . . . . . . .1951
*Caravan Creek* . . . . . . . . . . . . . . . . . . . . . . . . . . . . . . . .1954
*On Your Marks* (rev. ed.) . . . . . . . . . . . . . . . . . . . . . . . . .1954/1964
*The Light Blue Hills* . . . . . . . . . . . . . . . . . . . . . . . . . . . . .1959
"Why Do People Read Detective Stories?" in *Murder Ink* . . . . . . . . . . . . .1977

# 7
# Margery Allingham

Margery Allingham had been dead for more than two decades when, in 1988, the Public Broadcasting System starred Albert Campion, her detective, in a *Mystery!* series. This series revived interest in Allingham's detective stories, and as a result, many of her titles were reprinted.

Julia Thorogood's 1991 biography of Allingham makes numerous references to her diary entries and to papers and interviews of persons close to her. The author herself talked freely about her writing career.

Margery Louise Allingham (known to her family as Marge) was born in Ealing, England on May 20, 1904, to Herbert John Allingham and his cousin, Emily Jane (Hughes) Allingham. Margery described her family as second generation London Irish, pink in their politics. About her father she said, "I think he was the most impressive personality I ever met. I adored him." Herbert was the editor of the *Christian Globe*, a nonconformist weekly owned by his father; Herbert also ran the *London Journal* until he became a freelance writer for pulps. (On occasion, he produced a female detective to please his female readers.) His wife, considerably younger than he, was originally a milliner. A difficult and domineering woman, she did not want children. Moreover, she shared that information with Margery, dwelling much on the physical suffering caused her by the birth of her first child. Em, as she was known, soon joined her husband's profession, frequently contributing to magazines. Her sister, Maud Hughes, edited a magazine.

When Margery was a few months old, the family moved from their suburban London home to a converted rectory at Layer Breton on the Essex salt marshes. Although they kept an apartment in London, they had weekend visits from friends who were various kinds of writers. These writer friends of her father apparently took an interest in her and in some cases, kept in touch with her career.

It was her grandmother who taught her to read. According to Margery herself, "My father wrote, my mother wrote, all the weekend visitors wrote, and as soon as I could master the appallingly difficult business of making the initial marks, so did I." The family regarded writing as the only reasonable way to pass time and to earn a living.

It was not considered reasonable by a new housemaid who snatched a notebook from young Margery, exclaiming, "Master, Missus and three strangers all sitting in different rooms writing down LIES, and now you're starting!"

According to Margery, "When I was 7 years old my father began to train me to become a writer like himself. I was given a study of my own and a plot for a fairy story. Under his supervision I wrote and rewrote this story for nearly a year, at which time I began another." Although there was little warmth between Margery and her mother, and although her father was preoccupied most of the time, she grew up feeling that her father had some regard for her. Her first publication was in her grandfather's magazine. The piece was not edited, beginning "Once Apon a time...." When she was eight, she actually received some shillings for a story that appeared in a journal edited by her aunt.

In 1911, she was sent to a weekly boarding school in Colchester. She did not feel at home there, failing to learn spelling and other essentials. She also developed a stutter. After contracting typhoid fever, she spent a long period at home, when she was taught by governesses. Returning to Colchester, she remained there for most of World War I as a full boarder. In 1919, she attended a more modern and academic school in Cambridge. Here, too, she felt isolated and did not distinguish herself. (In adult life, she seemed to be antagonistic to school-mistress types.) She later claimed that educational influences on her included the writings of Robert Louis Stevenson, Shakespeare, particularly *Macbeth,* and the fairy stories of childhood.

Late in 1917, the house in Essex was abandoned; the family moved to London, retaining a house on Mersea Island, near Layer Breton.

By 1921, Margery was a published author. Her *Blackerchief Dick* was set in the 17th century and concerned smuggling and murder in Mersea Island. At first it was claimed that through seances she had received source material from the dead. Fortunately her husband later stated that these communications were "entirely the product of Margery's dynamic imagination." She maintained a keen interest in spiritualism and mental telepathy.

Before *Blackerchief Dick* came out, its author was a student of dramatic art at Regent Street Polytechnic. One reason for this was a desire

Margery Allingham in 1939 by Bessano. By courtesy of the National Portrait Gallery, London.

to overcome her stammering—and in this she was successful. While studying there, she wrote a drama in verse about Dido and Aeneas and had a student cast of 50 perform in it. The sets and also the book jacket of her first book were designed by Philip (Pip) Youngman Carter. He and Margery had heard of each other through their families—her father and his uncle had become close friends at Cambridge. The young people met in 1921 and were attracted to each other; for one thing, they had a mutual fondness of plays, and often went to performances together. It was Pip who persuaded Margery to drop the acting career she hoped for because he believed the competition was too stiff for her.

Margery spent an 18-month period in 1921–22 writing a book entitled *Green Corn*. Her father had suggested that she try to produce "a factual account of the innermost thoughts, aspirations, and actions of the young as you know them." Not surprisingly, the book was unpublishable; it was dreary because its author was part of a generation disillusioned by the tragedy if the Great War.

Allingham categorized her literary output as "right-hand" and "left-hand." She compared the first to the story one tells spontaneously at a party; here she could "coax the life out of herself onto the dead paper in any private way one pleases." The second—left-handed writing—had to conform to editorial requirements. In the 1920s and 1930s, to earn money, she did a considerable amount of left-handed writing. She managed this, for example, by making stories from silent movies for one of her aunt's enterprises, a magazine for girls. She also wrote original short stories and serials and produced nonfiction, such as reviews. The stories from silent movies ended with the advent of "talkies."

Mystery writing became attractive to her: "Nobody cared what the Mystery Writer thought, so long as he did his work and sold his story. It suited me." She looked on the mystery novel as a box with four sides—"a Killing, a Mystery, an Enquiring and a Conclusion with an Element of Satisfaction in it." She regarded her books "as novels, not just thrillers or detective stories." They represented right-hand stories and the opportunity to introduce humor or frivolity if she chose to, and she had decided that the serious nature of a conventional novel was too confining for her.

Allingham's first mystery novel was *The White Cottage Mystery*, published in 1927 as a serial for the *Daily Express*. The following year it appeared in book form. Its author, however, took little pride in it, later excluding it from lists of her published works.

That same year she married Pip, who was by then an accomplished commercial artist. Besides illustrating and designing book jackets, he at times held editorial positions. He noted that he loved her for her charm and gaiety, as well as her generosity and her kindness. She was fashion conscious and extremely deft with a needle. She moved gracefully, had brown eyes and dark hair and beautiful bone structure. However, all her adult life she battled being overweight—grossly overweight at times. This may have been in part due to thyroid dysfunction which was not always adequately controlled. The childless marriage had its ups and downs over time, and survived Pip's infidelity.

After a few years in London, the couple moved to Essex, retaining an apartment in London. By 1934, they were able to buy their own Queen Anne house in Tolleshunt D'Arcy on the Blackwater River. They entered into the life of the village, with Pip becoming a local cricket player. Allingham wrote: "...our life is typical of the English countryside. Horses, dogs, our garden, and village activities take up most of our leisure time." A litter of pups brought the total of their dogs to 14 at the end of 1934, and the garden afforded them great pleasure. At D'Arcy House the Carters entertained journalists, artists and the like, as did Margery's family. She was the chief breadwinner of the "Gang" that frequented her home. (One member, known as Grog, arrived shortly after the Allinghams were married, and stayed for 13 years, except for the time he served in the Royal Air Force during World War II.) At times Margery was under great stress to earn enough. Pip and Grog helped by often taking dictation from her and then typing up her stories. Family problems, including the death of her father in 1936, added to Margery's troubles. She experienced increasingly frequent periods of depression and a sense of deep exhaustion, but still managed to write.

Allingham introduced Albert Campion in *The Crime at Black Dudley* (1929). In this and the next two Campion mysteries she used "the plum pudding principle" of inserting as many incidents, jokes and imaginations as possible. Of her writing, she stated, "I have no particular ax to grind and I belong to no rigid school of thought...." (She called herself middle Church of England.) "Don Marquis is my favorite American author and the writers who have influenced me most in my life are, I should say, Shakespeare, Sterne and the elder Dumas." She thought that Christie had "the liveliest intelligence in the business." She admired Tey but was not fond of Sayers. She often discussed plots with Pip and conferred with him about her stories, especially at the beginning of her career. She considered bad writing and slovenly construction a "discourtesy to the reader." She did not find writing easy. She never learned to spell. It was not until 1940 that she taught herself to type. Nevertheless, she became a recognized author of the detective story genre, and her interest concentrated on East Anglia and London. In the 1930s, she wrote three novels under the pen name of Maxwell March. (She longed to write novels, but was not willing to risk the loss of her income from the sale of detective fiction.) One of her publishers, Dwye Evans, found her difficult to deal with, since she demanded praise, resented criticism and had, in his estimation, an inflated idea of her own abilities.

During World War II, with Essex a target for Nazi bombs and her husband serving in the Western Desert and Iraq, Allingham engaged in various stages of volunteer war work. She was particularly concerned with billeting evacuated children and pregnant women. Tolleshunt D'Arcy itself was bombed in October, 1940. Referring to the question that she had heard before in 1914—"Would I honestly die rather than give in?"—she came to the conclusion that mental and moral slavery was worse than death. *The Oaken Bucket* (1941), although fiction, described how her cohorts endured the early part of the war. Suggested by her American publisher, it was well received in the United States.

In 1949, with Pip, she was able to visit that country on business. Most people were still crossing the Atlantic by ship, but they chose to fly to New York via Iceland.

In 1956, Joyce Allingham moved into the Carter home and helped her sister with the business aspects of her writing career. Margery felt particularly harassed by the requirements regarding income taxes. Previously she had had to undergo electro-convulsive therapy for her emotional state. Her physical health was not good; she suffered from chronic bronchitis and sinusitis, not helped by her heavy smoking. An added burden was the care of geriatric relatives, a burden that Joyce shared with her. For 10 years, Margery had disregarded what turned out to be cancer of the breast. It took its toll on June 30, 1966. She was 62.

She left unfinished *Cargo of Eagles*, which her husband completed. He also wrote two Campion books on his own before he died in 1969. They were based on ideas he had discussed with his wife.

If Margery Allingham resented the position of the mystery story in literature, she appreciated the freedom it gave to writers of that genre. According to her, "We have the privileges of court fools. There is very little we dare not say in any company in any land."

Private detective Albert Campion appeared in Allingham's books from 1929 until 1968, and her fame rests on this series. The reader knows that Campion belonged to the nobility, although he was a younger son. Described as a tall, pale young man with blue eyes, sleek yellow hair, large horn-rimmed glasses and absurd falsetto drawl, he was, at first, regarded as "just a silly ass." But that impression changed. It appeared that Campion was a Cambridge man, even a collector of fine art. He had an interesting assistant, a reformed criminal named Magersfontein Lugg. Later (1949) Allingham introduced Charles Luke, a police detective. There was also a stalwart policeman named Stanislaus Oates. To add additional variety, Campion's sister, Valentine, was a dress designer. But the most important female in the series was the beautiful and elegant Lady Amanda Fitton, whom Campion ultimately married. She came on stage in *Sweet Danger* (1937), an 18-year-old redhead with unusual mechanical skills. Later she was an aircraft designer and in time, the mother of Rupert Campion, future Harvard student. Albert's associates added color to his drabness.

The series presented a variety of settings. *Flowers for the Judge* (1936) involved a publishing company and a trial. *Coroner's Pidgin* (1945) opened with a description of Lugg and Edna, Dowager Marchioness of Carados, delivering a dead woman to Campion's upstairs apartment. It developed that the night before Lady Carados' son was to be married, the dead woman was found in his bed. *Traitor's Purse* (1941) portrayed Campion with amnesia from a blow to his head involved in a plot to counter a Nazi scheme to induce the havoc of artificial inflation in his homeland. (It is intriguing that after the war, the plan for a similar scheme was revealed.) Allingham was adept at introducing into her writing contemporary issues of her day such as cold war spying and urban redevelopment. This was consistent with her belief that her books were novels "of the life of the time."

Her efforts brought her election to the famous Detection Club, along with many notable authors. *Hide My Eyes*, a Campion novel, brought its author a Silver Daggear.

Thanks to Margery Allingham's timeless imagination, future detective story fans will be as well entertained as their predecessors. Her skill as a writer in creating character and setting is exemplified by a fan letter she received in 1943. Written from a prisoner-of-war camp, it was sent to the fictional Albert Campion at his fictional address, 17A Bottle Street, London.

## *Listing of Works by Margery Allingham*

PSEUDONYMS: Maxwell March, Margery Allingham Carter

### ALBERT CAMPION SERIES

*The Crime at Black Dudley* . . . . . . . . . . . . . . . . . . . . . . . . . . . . . . . . . . 1929
(published in the U.S. as The *Black Dudley Murder*)
*Mystery Mile* . . . . . . . . . . . . . . . . . . . . . . . . . . . . . . . . . . . . . . . . . 1930

*Look to the Lady* . . . . . . . . . . . . . . . . . . . . . . . . . . . . . . .1931
(published in the U.S. as *The Gryth Chalice Murder*)
*Mystery Mile* . . . . . . . . . . . . . . . . . . . . . . . . . . . . . . . .1930
*Police at the Funeral* . . . . . . . . . . . . . . . . . . . . . . . . . . .1931
*Sweet Danger* . . . . . . . . . . . . . . . . . . . . . . . . . . . . . . . .1933
(published in the U.S. as *Kingdom of Death*)
*The Fear Sign* . . . . . . . . . . . . . . . . . . . . . . . . . . . . . . . .1933
*Death of a Ghost* . . . . . . . . . . . . . . . . . . . . . . . . . . . . . .1934
*Flowers for the Judge* . . . . . . . . . . . . . . . . . . . . . . . . . . .1936
(published in the U.S. as *Legacy in Blood*)
*Dancers in Mourning* . . . . . . . . . . . . . . . . . . . . . . . . . . .1937
(published in the U.S. as *Who Killed Chloe?*)
*The Case of the Late Pig* . . . . . . . . . . . . . . . . . . . . . . . . .1937
*The Fashion in Shrouds* . . . . . . . . . . . . . . . . . . . . . . . . . .1938
*Black Plumes* . . . . . . . . . . . . . . . . . . . . . . . . . . . . . . . .1940
*Traitor's Purse* . . . . . . . . . . . . . . . . . . . . . . . . . . . . . . .1941
(published in the U.S. as *The Sabotage Murder Mystery*)
*Coroner's Pidgin* . . . . . . . . . . . . . . . . . . . . . . . . . . . . . .1945
(published in the U.S. as *Pearls Before Swine*)
*More Work for the Undertaker* . . . . . . . . . . . . . . . . . . . . . .1949
*The Tiger in the Smoke* . . . . . . . . . . . . . . . . . . . . . . . . . .1952
*No Love Lost* . . . . . . . . . . . . . . . . . . . . . . . . . . . . . . . .1954
*The Beckoning Lady* . . . . . . . . . . . . . . . . . . . . . . . . . . . .1955
(published in the U.S. as *The Estate of the Beckoning Lady*)
*Ten Were Missing* . . . . . . . . . . . . . . . . . . . . . . . . . . . . . .1958
*The China Governess* . . . . . . . . . . . . . . . . . . . . . . . . . . . .1962
*The Mind Readers* . . . . . . . . . . . . . . . . . . . . . . . . . . . . . .1965
(with Philip Youngman Carter) *Cargo of Eagles* . . . . . . . . . . . . .1968
(by Philip Youngman Carter) *Mr. Campion's Farthing* . . . . . . . . . . .1969
(by Philip Youngman Carter) *Mr. Campion's Falcon*
(published in the U.S. as *Mr. Campion's Quarry*) . . . . . . . . . . . . .1970

## Books of Various Types

*Blackerchief Dick* . . . . . . . . . . . . . . . . . . . . . . . . . . . . . .1923
*Water in a Sieve* . . . . . . . . . . . . . . . . . . . . . . . . . . . . . .1925
*The White Cottage Mystery* . . . . . . . . . . . . . . . . . . . . . . . .1928
(with others) *Six Against the Yard* . . . . . . . . . . . . . . . . . . . .1936
(also published as *Six Against Scotland Yard*)
*Mr. Campion: Criminologist* . . . . . . . . . . . . . . . . . . . . . . . .1937
*Mr. Campion and Others* . . . . . . . . . . . . . . . . . . . . . . . . . .1939
*The Oaken Heart* . . . . . . . . . . . . . . . . . . . . . . . . . . . . . .1941
*Dance of the Years* . . . . . . . . . . . . . . . . . . . . . . . . . . . . .1943
(published in the U.S. as *The Gallantrys*)
*Wanted: Someone Innocent* . . . . . . . . . . . . . . . . . . . . . . . . .1946
*The Casebook of Mr. Campion* . . . . . . . . . . . . . . . . . . . . . . .1947

*Deadly Duo* . . . . . . . . . . . . . . . . . . . . . . . . . . . . . . . . . . . 1949, 1950
(also published as *Take Two at Bedtime*)
*Crime and Mr. Campion* . . . . . . . . . . . . . . . . . . . . . . . . . . . . . . 1959
*Three Cases for Mr. Campion* . . . . . . . . . . . . . . . . . . . . . . . . . . 1961
*The Mysterious Mr. Campion* . . . . . . . . . . . . . . . . . . . . . . . . . . 1963
*Mr. Campion's Lady* . . . . . . . . . . . . . . . . . . . . . . . . . . . . . . . . 1965
*Mr. Campion's Clowns* . . . . . . . . . . . . . . . . . . . . . . . . . . . . . . 1967

(Other omnibuses contain various works)

## Books by Maxwell March

*Other Man's Danger* . . . . . . . . . . . . . . . . . . . . . . . . . . . . . . . . 1933
(published in the U.S. as *The Man of Dangerous Secrets*)
*Rogues' Holiday* . . . . . . . . . . . . . . . . . . . . . . . . . . . . . . . . . . 1935
*The Shadow in the House* . . . . . . . . . . . . . . . . . . . . . . . . . . . . 1936

# 8

# Edith Pargeter

## *(Ellis Peters)*

After writing a number of books, Ellis Peters (Edith Pargeter) invented Brother Cadfael, a product of the 12th century. It is through the series about him that Peters remains a favorite with detective story readers.

She was born Edith Mary Pargeter on September 28, 1913, in Horsehay, Shropshire, England, the youngest of the three children of Edmund Valentine and Edith (Hordley) Pargeter. Her father was the head clerk and timekeeper at the local ironworks. Her mother was artistic, musical and "interested in everything." Raising her family and caring for her Welsh mother who lived with the Pargeters was not easy in their two-bedroom cottage that lacked utilities today considered essential. The author-to-be remembered that the house was full of books and music—little else—yet, she did not feel deprived.

In the 1920s, few families could afford to travel far, so Edith became familiar with the geography and history of her surroundings. "I was born and bred in Shropshire," Pargeter wrote, "and have never yet found any sound reason for leaving it, except perhaps for the pleasure of coming back to it again after forays into regions otherwise delightful in themselves, but no substitute for home" The nearest town was Shrewsbury, which she visited often as a young child when taken to an eye specialist. Three miles from Horsehay was Wellington, where her maternal uncle lived. Her cousins there were talented musically, and contact with them helped to foster in Edith an early appreciation of music—something that remained with her all her life.

Edith Pargeter by Roy Morgan. By courtesy of Deborah Owen Ltd.

Shropshire, bisected by the Severn River, is a border county (England and Wales) with history that dates back to the Romans. Once rich in iron ore and coal, it was the home of the Industrial Revolution, and abandoned forges contrasted with the rural scenery. Edith had childhood recollections of long walks with her mother through the countryside when they encountered ruins of abbeys.

When Edith began at the village school in Dawley, a mile from home, she could already read. While still in primary school, she expressed the desire to be a writer, and in this she was encouraged by a teacher named Donald Wase. She won a scholarship to Coalbrookdale High School for Girls in Ironbridge Gorge. There, she excelled in English, Latin, and history and again was encouraged to write, this time by a teacher named Ethel Harvey. At 15, she spent five pounds for a two-volume *History of Shrewsbury*, foreshadowing a longtime literary interest. Although she obtained an Oxford Higher School Certificate and first-class honors in English, she decided on a career in writing rather than a university degree.

Edith needed a job, but when she left school in 1930, she encountered a depressed economy. She finally became a pharmacist's assistant (referred to in England as chemist's assistant) in Dawley, and occupied the position for seven years.

Pargeter's literary career began early with the publication of short stories and a novel written under her name. Calling herself Jolyon Carr, she had several novels serialized in regional newspapers. She used two other pseudonyms before she became well known: John Redfern and Peter Benedict. Her first full-length novel, *The City Lies Foursquare,* came out in 1939 with the author listed as Edith Pargeter.

When Britain declared war in 1939, she tried to enlist in the air force. Since pharmacist's assistant was a "reserved occupation," she was not accepted. Resigning her position in Dawley, she listed herself as an author and made successful application to the Women's Royal Naval Service (WRNS). According to her, "authors were clearly expendable." But an author can type, and she found herself a teleprinter operator in the Signals Office. She spent most of the war in Liverpool, which sustained heavy bombing in 1941—on one particular night the Luftwaffe dropped 50,000 incendiary devices and 363 tons of explosives. Edith was part of a group of women who monitored a direct transatlantic line with Newfoundland, from where Allied convoys sailed.

Being in the military did not deter Pargeter from writing; she was able to concentrate with table tennis going on in one end of the common room and a piano playing in the other. Her works for the war years included *She Goes to War* (1942), a trilogy about the war consisting of

*The Eighth Champion of Christendom* (1945), *Reluctant Odyssey* (1946), and *Warfare Accomplished* (1947). It was well received and demonstrated that its author had a social conscience. In 1944, she received the British Empire Medal "for zeal in whole-hearted devotion to duty." She was demobilized on V-J Day as Petty Officer.

Returning to Shropshire, Pargeter lived with her mother until the latter's death in 1956. (Her father had died 16 years before.) Then she and her engineer brother Edmund Ellis, but known as Ellis, bought an 18th century house in Madeley, remaining there for 35 years. Neither married. She was firm in her decision that writing was the overriding importance in her life. The siblings shared similar opinions about values; for instance, they expended much energy on an ultimately unsuccessful venture to establish the Shropshire Adult College.

In an interview in 1947, Pargeter noted how the war had changed the role of women: it was no longer necessary for them to assert that they are the equals of men; nor does this in any way diminish the stature of man—it is a means to establish a new and better balanced relationship in which both find full scope.

Pargeter developed a deep interest in the people and literature of Czechoslovakia. According to Lewis, this interest began in 1938 when British Prime Minister Neville Chamberlain secured the cession of Sudetenland to Germany by the Czechoslovaks. The Munich Pact she considered the betrayal of an ally, although it was intended to be in the interests of "peace in our time." While in uniform, she came into contact with many people from Czechoslovakia. When the war was over, she and Ellis visited that country as part of an international summer school. This led to her reading and translating poetry and prose written in Czechoslovakian. Various translations by her of that literature were published between 1957 and 1970. Through her Czech contacts, she paid a long visit to India.

Pargeter's detection writing was launched with *Fallen Into the Pit* (1951), which presented the Felse family. The award-winning *Death and the Joyful Woman* did not appear until 11 years after the first in the series, and with it Pargeter began to write as Ellis Peters. She continued to use that pseudonym for the remaining 11 books in the Ellis Peters series.

The 20-book Cadfael series began with *A Morbid Taste for Bones* (1977) and ended with *Brother Cadfael's Penance* (1994), all written as Ellis Peters, the pen name Pargeter intended for mysteries. It, of course, honored her brother.

Pargeter characterized herself essentially a storyteller, "and in my view, no one who can't make that statement can possibly be a novelist, the novel being by definition an extended narrative reflecting the human condition, with the accent on the word 'narrative.'" She claimed that the works of Rudyard Kipling, Thomas Mallory, and Helen Waddell were among those that influenced her writing.

In September, 1995, a stroke paralyzed most of the right side of her body. Previous to that, she had suffered a broken back and had undergone partial amputation of one leg. She died on October 14, 1995, at 82.

Pargeter was the recipient of many honors. Besides an Edgar Award, she won a Silver Dagger Award (*Monk's Hood*) and the Diamond Dagger Award for lifetime achievement from the British Crime Writers' Association. In 1994, she was awarded an Order of the British Empire in the Queen's New Years Honours List. The same year, Birmingham University bestowed an honorary Master of Arts. The honor that pleased her most was the Gold Medal (1968) of the Czechoslovak Society for International Relations, recognizing her contributions to Czech literature. It was recommended by the Czechoslovak Writers' Union.

In a posthumous tribute, Sue Feder, an authority on Peters, noted that the famous author treated us to ancient Rome, medieval Shrewsbury, contemporary India and Czechoslovakia; she conducted trips to the sea, the mountains, Venice; she focused our attention on border skirmishes, a continuing civil war, World War II; she wrote about archeology, opera and heresy; through her we met kings and common soldiers, artists, writers, musicians, singers, criminals—smart and stupid—the occasional witch, a vicious Nazi, and more.

Pargeter's first series featured the Felse family of Shropshire and presented a variety of entertaining situations. George, the father, was a detective-sergeant in the county C.I.D. and rose through the ranks as the series progressed. He represented the traditional British police investigator. Bunty, his wife, was a retired opera singer. Dominic, their son, made his first appearance at 13 and later was seen as an undergraduate at Oxford. He was 16 in *Death and the Joyful Woman* and solved a murder. Peters described him as "tallish, pleasant-looking, reasonably extrovert, healthily certain of himself, taking himself a bit seriously at this stage...."

Cadfael was Pargeter's most important character. His chronicles are fiction based on historical events and the result of extensive historical research. Peters contended, "You must respect documented fact—only when the authorities fight over details do I use my own judgment and make a mix with fiction." In 1975, the National Library of Wales edited and published the entire Cartulary of Shrewsbury Abbey, and this was one of the many sources Pargeter used.

Cadfael was born in Trefriw, in Gwynedd, Wales, in 1180. By the age of 14, he was working for an English wool-merchant in Shrewsbury. Cadfael was good with the short bow and took kindly to the sword. According to himself: "The best of my following years were spent in Shrewsbury, I know it like my own palm, abbey and all. My master sent me there a year and more, to get my letters. But I quit that service when he died. I'd pledged nothing to the son, and he was a poor shadow of his father. That was when I took the Cross...."

As part of the First Crusade, he was present at the sieges of Antioch, Ascalon and Jerusalem. Later he became captain of a fishing boat. It was not until 1120 that he returned to England. Pargeter explained this as follows: "My monk had to be a man of wide worldly experience and an inexhaustible fund of resigned tolerance for the human condition. His crusading and seafaring past, with all its enthusiasms and disillusionments, was referred to from the beginning...."

After his return home, Cadfael soon entered the Rule of St. Benedict in the Abbey of St. Peter and St. Paul at Shrewsbury. However, when first introduced to readers (*A Morbid Taste for Bones*), he was "seventeen years tonsured"; he answered to Abbot Heribert and later to Father Radulfan. Nevertheless, Cadfael sometimes broke rules if it benefited others. He was not a priest; he could not hear confession or deliver the Sacraments. Brother Cadfael's accomplishments were considerable. He proved to be an apothecary and physician. This entailed tending his herb garden, preparing medicines and providing for a leper hospital. Through such activities, he maintained contact with persons outside the abbey; persons such as Hugh Beringar, the Sheriff of Shropshire.

In the secular world, a violent war was in progress as Stephen, King of England from 1135 to 1154, struggled to retain his throne, and the war affected Cadfael. *Brother Cadfael's Presence* exemplifies the interest Pargeter is able to raise and sustain. The monk had learned that he had a son, Olivier de Bretagne, whose Syrian mother, Miriam, was a young widow whom Cadfael, "a brave and kind English soldier," met in Antioch. (There is a hint of this in *Monk's Hood* when Cadfael "did wonder if he had left printings of himself somewhere in the world.") When Olivier was taken prisoner in battle, Cadfael broke his monastic vow by going to find him and offering his own life for his son's release. Both escaped to freedom. Cadfael also saved another soldier unjustly accused of murder, and did this by producing the real culprit. With his son delivered from danger, Cadfael returned to the abbey.

Author Andrew Greeley noted that Pargeter makes us know the monks and townsfolk and squires and nobility, almost as if they were friends and neighbors—despite a separation of eight centuries.

This was Pargeter's intention. She once said, "I almost feel that I'm building up a picture of medieval Shrewsbury with the craftsmen and the merchants and weavers … and that I've made it a real community. I want to go on doing this. Part of my life is indeed involved in Cadfael's community and I hope I've succeeded in passing this along to the readers." She claimed that the writing of the Cadfael novels had given her more pleasure that anything else she had done. "Cadfael opens channels for me to say, through him, things it would be difficult to say through a modern protagonist." The Cadfael books have been translated into 20 languages; a British Broadcasting Corporation television series starring Sir Derek Jakobi was produced.

Cadfael fans in droves visit the Shrewsbury Quest, an attraction based on medieval England and the monastic life in particular. Pargeter was an ardent supporter of this.

Shrewsbury Abbey itself, more than 900 years old, has appealed to Cadfael fans to donate funds for its restoration.

## *Listing of Works by Edith Pargeter*

PSEUDONYMS: Jolyon Carr, John Redfern, Peter Benedict, Ellis Peters

### BROTHER CADFAEL SERIES (AS ELLIS PETERS)

*A Morbid Taste for Bones* . . . . . . . . . . . . . . . . . . . . . . . . . . . .1977
*One Corpse Too Many* . . . . . . . . . . . . . . . . . . . . . . . . . . . .1979
*Monk's Hood* . . . . . . . . . . . . . . . . . . . . . . . . . . . . . . . . .1980
*The Leper of St. Giles* . . . . . . . . . . . . . . . . . . . . . . . . . . . .1981
*St. Peter's Fair* . . . . . . . . . . . . . . . . . . . . . . . . . . . . . . .1981
*The Virgin in the Ice* . . . . . . . . . . . . . . . . . . . . . . . . . . . .1982
*The Devil's Novice* . . . . . . . . . . . . . . . . . . . . . . . . . . . . .1983
*The Sanctuary Sparrow* . . . . . . . . . . . . . . . . . . . . . . . . . . .1983
*The Dead Man's Ransom* . . . . . . . . . . . . . . . . . . . . . . . . . .1984
*The Pilgrim of Hate* . . . . . . . . . . . . . . . . . . . . . . . . . . . . .1984
*An Excellent Mystery* . . . . . . . . . . . . . . . . . . . . . . . . . . . .1985
*The Raven in the Foregate* . . . . . . . . . . . . . . . . . . . . . . . . .1986
*The Rose Rent* . . . . . . . . . . . . . . . . . . . . . . . . . . . . . . . .1986
*The Hermit of Eyton Forest* . . . . . . . . . . . . . . . . . . . . . . . .1987
*The Confession of Brother Haluin* . . . . . . . . . . . . . . . . . . . .1988
*The Heretic's Apprentice* . . . . . . . . . . . . . . . . . . . . . . . . . .1989
*The Potter's Field* . . . . . . . . . . . . . . . . . . . . . . . . . . . . . .1989
*Summer of the Danes* . . . . . . . . . . . . . . . . . . . . . . . . . . . .1991

*The Holy Thief* .................................... 1992
*Brother Cadfael's Penance* .................................... 1994

FELSE FAMILY SERIES
(ALL EXCEPT FIRST AS ELLIS PETERS)

*Fallen into the Pit* .................................... 1951
*Death and the Joyful Woman* .................................... 1962
*Flight of a Witch* .................................... 1964
*A Nice Derangement of Epitaphs* .................................... 1965
(published in the U.S. as *Who Lies Here?*)
*The Piper on the Mountain* .................................... 1966
*Black is the Colour of My True Love's Heart* .................................... 1967
*The Grass-Widow's Tale* .................................... 1968
*The House of Green Turf* .................................... 1969
*Mourning Raga* .................................... 1969
*The Knocker on Death's Door* .................................... 1970
*Death to the Landlords!* .................................... 1972
*City of Gold and Shadows* .................................... 1973
*Rainbow's End* .................................... 1978

ROMANCE AND HISTORICAL WORKS

*Hortensius, Friend of Nero* .................................... 1936
*Iron-Bound* .................................... 1936
*The City Lies Foursquare* .................................... 1939
*Ordinary People* .................................... 1941
(published in the U.S. as *People of My Own*)
*She Goes to War* .................................... 1942
War trilogy:
*The Eigth Champion of Christendom* .................................... 1946
*Reluctant Odyssey* .................................... 1946
*Warfare Accomplished* .................................... 1947
*By Firelight* .................................... 1948
(published in the U.S. as *By This Strange Fire*)
*The Fair Young Phoenix* .................................... 1948
*Lost Children* .................................... 1950
*Holiday with Violence* .................................... 1952
*Most Loving Mere Folly* .................................... 1953
*This Rough Magic* .................................... 1953
*The Soldier at the Door* .................................... 1954
*A Means of Grace* .................................... 1956
*The Heaven Tree* .................................... 1960
*The Green Branch* .................................... 1962
*The Scarlet Seed* .................................... 1963
*A Bloody Field by Shrewsbury* .................................... 1972
(published in the U.S. as *The Bloody Field*)

Brothers of Gwynedd quartet:
*Sunrise in the West* . . . . . 1974
*The Dragon of Noonday* . . . . . 1975
*The Hounds of Sunset* . . . . . 1976
*Afterglow and Nightfall* . . . . . 1977
*The Marriage of Meggotta* . . . . . 1979

### Other Works (as Ellis Peters)

*Death Mask* . . . . . 1960
*Where There's a Will* . . . . . 1960
(published in England as *The Will and the Deed;* a second U.S. issue has the same title)
*Funeral of Figaro* . . . . . 1962
*The Horn of Roland* . . . . . 1974
*Never Pick up Hitch-Hikers!* (bound with works of other authors) . . . . . 1976

### Short Stories

*The Assize of the Dying* . . . . . 1958
*The Lily Hand and Other Sories* (as Ellis Peters) . . . . . 1965
*A Rare Benedictine* . . . . . 1988

### Nonfiction

*The Coast of Bohemia* . . . . . 1950
*Shropshire* (with Ray Morgan) . . . . . 1992
*Strongholds and Sanctuaries* (with Ray Morgan) . . . . . 1993

### Novels (as Peter Benedict)

*Day Star* . . . . . 1937

### Novels (as Jolyon Carr)

*Murder in the Dispensary* . . . . . 1938
*Freedom for Two* . . . . . 1939
*Masters of the Parachute Mail* . . . . . 1940
*Death Comes by Post* . . . . . 1940

### Translations from the Czech

*Tales of the Little Quarter* (by Jan Neruda) . . . . . 1957
*Don Juan* (by Joseph Toman) . . . . . 1958
*A Handful of Linden Leaves: An Anthology of Czech Poetry* . . . . . 1958

*The Sorrowful and Heroic Life of John Amos Comenius* (by Frantisek Kosik) . . . . . . . . . . . . . . . .1958
*The Abortionists* (by Valja Styblova) . . . . . . . . . . . . . . . . . . . . . . . . . . . . . .1961
*Granny: Scenes from Country Life* (by Bozena Nemcova) . . . . . . . . . . . . . .1962
*The Linden Tree: An Anthology of Czech and Slovak Literature, 1890–1960* (by Mojmir Otruba and Zdenek Pesat, eds.) . . . . . . . . . . . .1962
*Legends of Old Bohemia* (by Alois Jirasek) . . . . . . . . . . . . . . . . . . . . . . . .1963
*The Terezin Requiem* (by Joseph Bor) . . . . . . . . . . . . . . . . . . . . . . . . . . .1963
*The End of the Old Times* (by Vladislav Vancura) . . . . . . . . . . . . . . . . . . . .1965
*May* (by Karel Hynek Macha) . . . . . . . . . . . . . . . . . . . . . . . . . . . . . . . . . .1965
*A Close Watch on the Trains* (by Bohumil Hrabel) . . . . . . . . . . . . . . . . . . . .1968
*Report on My Husband* (by Josefa Slanska) . . . . . . . . . . . . . . . . . . . . . . . . .1969
*Mozart in Prague* (by Jaroslav Seibert) . . . . . . . . . . . . . . . . . . . . . . . . . . .1970
*A Ship Named Hope: Two Novels* (by Ivan Klima) . . . . . . . . . . . . . . . . . . . .1970

(Contributor to various magazines)

# 9
# Phyllis Dorothy James White
## *(P.D. James)*

P.D. James (Phyllis Dorothy James White) began her first book when she was 39, working on it for three years. It was published when she was 42—a somewhat advanced age for an aspiring author. Unusual also was the fact that James had reached publication without rejection of that or any previous book.

Phyllis Dorothy James was born on August 3, 1920, in Oxford, England to Sidney Victor and Dorothy May (Hone) James. The former was a tax officer and the family middle class; an adult James declared herself a member of the Church of England but of no political party. She attended Cambridge Girls' School from 1931 to 1937. With regard to a university education, she once noted that her father was not disposed to educate girls. Money was needed because, at that time, higher education was not subsidized by the British government. Thus, Phyllis' formal education ended at the secondary school level. Nevertheless, she is well educated. A reader, she is a great admirer of Jane Austen and holds authors Waugh, Hardy, and Trollope in high regard. She also likes the poetry of George Crabbe and is knowledgeable about architecture.

At an early age, Phyllis expressed a desire to write. Her delayed development as an author was influenced by both family and world events.

Her first job was at a local tax office, where she worked for a year. Then she became assistant stage manager at the Festival Theatre in Cambridge.

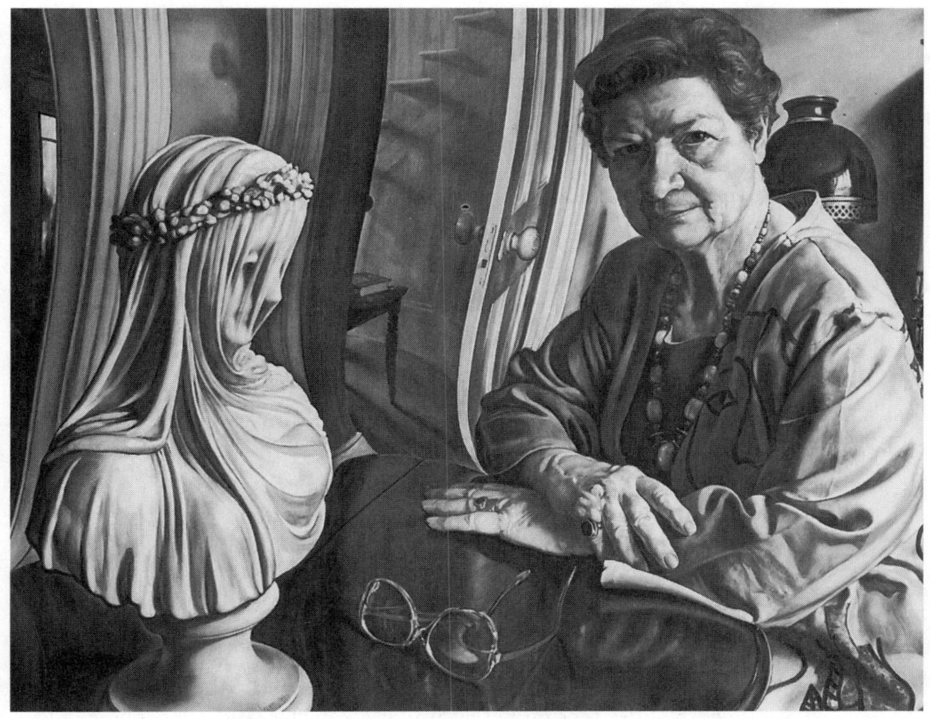

**Phyllis Dorothy James White in 1996 by Michael Taylor. By courtesy of the National Portrait Gallery, London.**

The Second World War broke out when she was 19. "You don't start a novel when you don't know if you're going to see the morning," she once said. In 1941, she left her job at the theater to marry Ernest Connor Bantry White, then a medical student. During the war, he served in the armed forces, and she worked as a Red Cross nurse and at the Ministry of Foods. Their daughter Clare was born in 1942 and Jane in 1944. In 1945, Dr. White was discharged from the military, seriously ill with schizophrenia. He lived until 1964, often incapacitated.

White once explained her situation: "...I had to look after him and two children and find a good safe job that would really bring in a wage check." In 1949, she joined the National Health Service, working in London, where most of her adult life has been spent. She finally worked up to the position of hospital administrator. To broaden her horizons, as she put it, in 1968, she sought employment in the Criminal Division of the British Home Office, and passed a highly competitive examination for placement at a senior level. She served there until 1979, becoming a specialist in juvenile delinquency. There she was in daily contact with police officials, judges and other personnel On retirement, she devoted herself to full-time writing.

In an interview in 1976, she said:

> Government *is* interesting; it brings me, though I'm not a *very* senior civil servant, in touch with Ministers of the Crown. It gives me an entree into the House of Commons and into the House of Lords during debates, and I see how policy is made. All this is fascinating to a writer. I think I'd been the poorer without it, but I like to think of myself as a writer who is also a civil servant.

White was in her mid–30s when she realized that being occupied with family and job meant "there is never an absolutely propitious time to starting down to write." She resolved to devote herself to writing between 6:00 and 8:00 A.M.—and stuck to that.

Why did she choose to write mystery fiction? According to her, she had always enjoyed reading mysteries, and cited Dorothy L. Sayers as a potent early influence:

> I thought I might be able to write a mystery rather well; I reasoned that such a popular genre might have the best chance of acceptance by a publisher; and I saw the writing of detective fiction with its challenging discipline, its inner tension between plot, character, and atmosphere, and its necessary reliance on structure and form as the best possible apprenticeship for a serious novelist.

In 1962, *Cover Her Face* appeared, with the author listed as P.D. James. With that name she would be judged by what she wrote, not by her sex. Incidentally, she was known as Mrs. White at work. The book was a classic mystery, which is described by Siebenheller as a crime presented, several suspects, various clues and a detective adept at finding, analyzing and interpreting. The detective's name was Adam Dalgliesh. *A Mind to Murder* followed the next year, and a Dalgliesh series was begun.

Ten years after the introduction of Dalgliesh, *An Unsuitable Job for a Woman,* by James, presented Cordelia Gray, another important character. By 1995, the former hospital administrator was the author of 13 books. Her works include short stories, essays, criticism and nonfiction; her play, *A Private Treason*, was first produced in 1985. Six of her books have been filmed and broadcast on British and American television. She has served as a magistrate and governor of the British Broadcasting Company. Critics have noted the accuracy of her backgrounds and the realism of her situations—a reflection of the experiences of her working life.

Her honors are many, including three Silver Daggers and a Diamond Dagger for lifetime achievement. She received the Order of the British Empire in 1983, and she was accepted into the Royal Society of Authors four years later. In 1991, a lifetime barony was created, and she is now Baroness James of Holland Park. As Phyllis White she is a grandmother several times. How would she like to be remembered? She told Jane Baderman:

> As a human being, I should like to be remembered as one who enhanced the pleasure in life for other people. I don't mean that I *am* that sort of human being, but that people, when they looked back at me, would want to smile or to laugh. And that my children would want to look back at me and feel that they had been happier because I'd been their mother.
>
> I think as a writer, I would like to be remembered as an honest and original craftsman, who was able to give pleasure, and entertainment, and release from the anxieties of our violent world to a large number of people—and to have troubled to try and do it well.

Adam Dalgliesh is James' most famous character. When the reader first meets him, he is an experienced Scotland Yard police officer with the rank of detective chief inspector. Well educated and a published poet, he is serious, controlled and introspective, concentrating on the problem at hand. He demands results, and he is honest: "I can't suppress evidence or omit relevant facts from my report because I don't choose to like them." His hunches are good, interrogation is important to him, and he seeks out such people as cleaning women and servants as well as suspects. His investigations involve him in a variety of areas, exemplified by the British hospital system, a writers' colony, a training school for nurses, forensic pathology, and the world of law courts. He is against capital punishment because he remembers mistakes that he has made. Dalgliesh is highly respected in his profession, and it is not surprising that he is soon promoted to superintendent and later to commander. (James is not confronted with the problem Christie had with Poirot—Dalgliesh ages as the series progresses.)

Details about Dalgliesh's personal life are scant. The son of a parson, he keeps in touch with an aunt named Jane Dalgliesh, from whom he ultimately inherits. He had lost his wife in childbirth and his newborn son at the same time. Thereafter, he seemed afraid to care for anyone. He shows interest in Deborah Risque, a young widow, but after some time, she decides to end the situation. He is referred to as handsome and described as dark, very tall, and loose-limbed.

White has said that Dalgliesh reflects many of her views and attitudes on life, and that she has a sympathy for him; she would not continue to write about a man she did not admire or at least sympathize with. She perceives her detective as:

> ...a very detached man, essentially a very lonely man in a lonely profession, one which brings him into contact with tragedy, with *evil*. At the same time, he has the sensitivity of a poet, which I think makes him a complex character and the reconciliation of these two very different facets of his character is interesting.

Another type of sleuth is Cordelia Gray, who inherits "a private enquiry firm" from her late partner, Bernie Pryde. Pryde is an ex-Meteropolitan policeman who once worked under Dalgliesh (and did not distinguish himself although his hero-worship of his chief was intense). Cordelia's chronically absent father was an itinerant Marxist poet and an amateur revolutionary. Brought up in foster homes and in a Catholic convent, she is young and inexperienced, but bright and likable. Unfortunately, the agency is sometimes reduced to tracing animals rather than persons. Dalgliesh's and Cordelia's paths cross at times. On their first encounter, she was pleased that he had credited her with his own brand of intelligence—she had behaved as he would have behaved. But she had also withheld from him some important information, something he suspected but could not prove. Moreover, he did not approve of such conduct. She believed that the circumstances justified her action.

In *The Black Tower* (1977) there is a hint of future relations between Gray and Dalgliesh, despite a considerable age difference. However, two years later, James wrote a piece about the situation, explaining that she had no plans to marry Dalgliesh to anyone. At the same time, she admitted that occasionally the best-regulated characters can escape from the sensible and controlling hand of their author, to embark on their own love life. (With regard to the present work, Dalgliesh is the first investigator whose creator is alive at the time of writing and therefore in a position to control the character's actions.)

Early in 2000, White revealed in a radio interview that Dalgliesh will finally fall in love in the book she expects to complete the following year. She admitted that presenting him as a widower was somewhat cowardly. "But I felt that in the detective novel you are coping with one great absolute which is death. I am not sure that at the same time you can cope with another great absolute, which is love."

James refers to many contemporary and historical events and issues of the 20th century. Here is a sampling. *A Mind to Murder* (1963) mentions LSD (lysergic acid diethylamide), a psychotomimetic drug not well known in the early part of the century. *Unnatural Causes* (1967) uses the word "queer" for "gay." *Shroud for a Nightingale* (1971) refers to the Nuremberg trials of 1946. A 1972 James book makes reference to ecology and molecular biology. In 1982, her fictional focus concerns avoiding Britain's high tax rate. A 1989 book revolves around a nuclear reactor, and AIDS is mentioned.

*Original Sin* (1994) is set in a publishing firm on the Thames. Dalgliesh is called in when the new managing editor is found dead. The murder's motive turns out to be revenge against a Frenchman who sold out to the Nazis during World War II. The characters are interesting, including Detective Inspector Kate Miskin who is a real professional devoted to her career. Suspense is maintained throughout. It seems to the writer that *Original Sin* approaches being a serious novel—and that is just what P.D. James wanted when she began to write a mystery.

## *Listing of Works by Phyllis Dorothy James White*

PSEUDONYM: P.D. James (used for all her books)

### ADAM DALGLIESH SERIES

*Cover Her Face* .......................................... 1962
*A Mind to Murder* .......................................... 1963
*Unnatural Causes* .......................................... 1967
*Shroud for a Nightingale* .......................................... 1971
*The Black Tower* .......................................... 1975
*Death of an Expert Witness* .......................................... 1986
*A Taste for Death* .......................................... 1986
*Devices and Desires* .......................................... 1989
*Original Sin* .......................................... 1994
*A Certain Justice* .......................................... 1997

### CORDELIA GRAY SERIES

*An Unsuitable Job for a Woman* .......................................... 1972
*The Skull Beneath the Skin* .......................................... 1982

### OTHER NOVELS

*Innocent Blood* .......................................... 1980
*The Children of Men* .......................................... 1992

## Nonfiction

(with Thomas A. Critchley) *The Maul and the Pear Tree: The Ratcliffe Highway Murders, 1811* . . . . . . . . . . . . . . . . . . . . . . . . . . . . . . . . . . . 1971
*Time to Be in Earnest* (an autobiography) . . . . . . . . . . . . . . . . . . . . . . . . . . . 2000

(Works appear in several omnibus volumes)

(Contributor to various crime publications)

# 10

# Gwendoline Butler
## *(Jennie Melville)*

Gwendoline Butler has the ability to write as convincingly about events that took place in the Victorian era as about events that happened after 1950.

She was born on August 19, 1920, in London to Alfred Edward Williams and Alice (Lee) Williams. Herself one of a set of twins, Gwendoline also had twin brothers. Apart from *Pickwick Papers,* the first book that she remembers reading was *The Mystery of the Yellow Room,* the translation of a famous French mystery. This led to her love of mysteries and detective stories. The years 1934 to 1942 saw her at Haberdashers' Aske's Hatchem Girls' School in London.

Wanting to be a historian, Gwendoline read medieval history at Lady Margaret Hall, Oxford from 1944 to 1949 and taught briefly at two Oxford colleges. In 1949, she married Lionel Butler, a professor in her field. They had one daughter, Lucilla.

According to Butler, when she decided to try writing as a profession, she fell naturally into a detective story. She loved the early Ellery Queen and Elizabeth Daly, but was not fond of Agatha Christie. Her first book was published in 1956, and her productivity since has been impressive. She writes novels—historical and otherwise; the John Coffin and the Charmian Daniels series have been popular. The latter is written under the pen name Jennie Melville.

Butler once made this comment:

> I have always thought of crime writers as entertainers, and I always desired to show that evil is punished even if not always by the law. I

> have also tried to show my characters in a bright light, like a stage spotlight, but against a dark, even menacing background.

*A Coffin for Pandora* won a Silver Dagger in 1973. In 1980, *The Red Staircase* was awarded the Romantic Novelists Association prize. Their author is a fellow of the Royal Society of Arts.

The Butlers once lived in St. Andrews, Scotland, where he taught medieval history at the university there. He died in 1983. She now lives in Surrey.

With a demanding writing schedule, Butler cannot spend much time on hobbies. She walks, swims, enjoys picture galleries and travels a bit, although not as much as when her husband was alive. As might be expected, she reads widely, including contemporary fiction. Her advice to new writers is, "Write and never be put down by publishers or reviewers. Keep at it." Butler has done a little television writing, which she says is much like writing a novel.

She says that in another life, she would have liked to go to a school of drama. This is because she would have liked to write plays, and believes that experience in living theater is needed, whether or not one has acting potential. Gwendoline Butler, approaching 80, still loves to write, enjoys making sentences and spinning stories. She will go on as long as she is published—*that* she needs, she said.

John Coffin first appeared in detective fiction in 1957. This sleuth was born in South London. His was not a happy childhood. His father disappeared; he remembers little of his mother. He was brought up by a grandmother and an aunt and then by an aunt alone; finally he was placed in foster homes. He did receive what appears to be a fair education at the Roan Boys' School.

Coffin served in World War II. He just missed being killed by a mortar shell but made a good recovery. After demobilization, he joined the Metropolitan Police force, starting his career as a constable in Greenwich, the borough long associated with longitude and timekeeping. Blessed with strong common sense and insatiable curiosity, he was well suited to his profession. He was soon promoted to the C.I.D., and advancement after advancement followed. He finally became head of the police in the newly created Second City of London.

The Second City is the fictional locale of London's Docklands along the Thames River. It is made up of the old boroughs with authentic-sounding names: Spinnergate, Leathergate, Swinehouse and East Hyde. These areas had seen many occupants of the land, among them Anglo-Saxons, Vikings and Normans. Now new immigrants live there with fam-

**Gwendoline Butler in 1993 by Kinsella Studio Lab. By courtesy of Gwendoline Butler.**

ilies whose ancestors had lived there for centuries. Some are rich, some poor. The district includes several hospitals, a university, many schools, churches, numerous bookmakers' stores, an illegal gambling house, two brothels. The Development Board had instituted a new police force, independent of the Metropolitan Police and of the City of London, to enforce the Queen's Peace. As chief commander, Coffin does this—so successfully that there are rumors that the next Honours List could bring him a peerage—lifetime, to be sure, but still a peerage. He enjoys his authority, despite the great responsibility it entails. No matter how many employees he has in his charge, he manages to keep old friends and is still a working detective; in fact, his code name is WALKER.

Coffin is an attractive figure throughout the series. He has many interests—history, genealogy, cricket, theater, to name a few. Tall and slender, he has broad shoulders, his eyes are blue; graying—and he does age—becomes him.

His personal life is not as exemplary as his professional career. A disastrous marriage is often in his thoughts; he has guilt about the death of their son. There had been drunkenness. However, that is under control, and he understands his vulnerability in that area.

For many years, Coffin has known a beautiful actress known Stella Pinero, whom he marries late in the series. Her dog Bob and his cat Tiddles are part of the family. His interest in genealogy brings him to Laetitia Bingham, his half-sister, rich and an international lawyer. He also discovers a half-brother, William, who lives in Edinburgh.

Letty owns St. Luke's Mansions complex, where she had bought an old Victoria church and developed from it three apartments, one of which Coffin bought. (It is in the tower, and from it can be seen the Thames, Tower Bridge and the top of St. Paul's Cathedral.) The main church became an in-the-round theater and she established a theater workshop on the rest of her land.

William was in possession of a diary written by the mother of the three. It recounts so many adventures that some thought is given to publishing it; the hope is that it might attract someone interested in making a film. On reading in the diary that his mother received a diamond tiara from a man said to be a Romanov, Coffin wonders how much of the diary is fiction. It had been assumed that the mother was dead, but the unpredictability she manifests in the diary provides the possibility that she will appear sometime.

The Second City that Butler represents is conducive to the making of good plots and intriguing characters. Incidentally, in 1988, she heard a Memorial Lecture in which it was suggested that a Second City of London could aid the economic and social regeneration of the Docklands. Fascinated with the idea, she created that world for her leading detective. In it there are a great variety of thieves, housebreakers, pickpockets, sneak thieves, prostitutes, rapists and murderers. There are also university people—as in *Cracking Open a Coffin*—and theater people—as in *Coffin in the Museum of Crime.* The introduction of Stella provides great opportunity for the discussion of theater productions. If the plots are sometimes overly complex, the settings provide much interest.

When first presented in 1962, Charmian Daniels is 27. She was born in Dundee, Scotland. Despite her family's poverty, she is a graduate of Glasgow University, where she studied social science. This introduced her to Sir Robert Peel and penal reform, with the ultimate result that she decided on a career in the police force.

After working in a secretarial position, she was a trainee constable pounding the streets in St. Andrews and Dundee, then a sergeant with the C.I.D. at Deerham Hills, near London. It was a banner day in her life when she bought her first car, a green baby Austin. She advanced, via London and the Met, to become head of a crime registry whose function is to coordinate all the records of crime in an area, excluding London, but the Met has to liaise with her. This offers many possibilities for solving complex cases. She also has accumulated files on local people—files that prove very useful. Daniels' hard-working and often short-handed unit is based in Windsor, where she lives; she has a sub-office in Slough.

Daniels has light reddish hair, big brown eyes and is attractive. According to her (writing in the first person), she thinks she has lost her Scottish accent; she is tall and physically fit enough to down a man who intends to kill her; she is brave, thorough in her work and sometimes has valuable flashes of insight; tact is not her forte; she looks for loyalty in friends and colleagues; she is ambitious. She believes that a policewoman should keep her maiden name; she likes to split the cost when she eats out with a man. Although her career identifies her with authority, she has charity and love.

Daniels' first marriage is to a colleague named Rupert Ascham. He is 15 years older than she and a widower with a son. Rupert dies when his wife is 37.

Daniels is clearly interested in her profession, and there are hints that more promotions are in store. She appears to be less interested in domestic pursuits. There have been men in her life, including her stepson; she still has relatives and friends in Scotland; her goddaughter Kate dies having a baby, but Charmain stays in contact with the family; she has an aged cat named Muff that affords her company. But as she approaches middle age, there are times when she is really lonesome. Probably this is why she marries her good friend Humphrey. Since he has an inherited title, she is sometimes correctly addressed as "Your Ladyship."

The opinion of a subordinate, Superintendent Henry Gervaine Horris—known as HG—is illuminating. He does not truly resent Daniels or dislike her personally; his anger is routine and would have been vented at any woman with more power than he had; his reaction is shared by more than half the force. He knows that she is honest, thorough and straightforward. And when HG's favorite granddaughter wants to join the police force, her grandfather recommends that she adopt Charmian Daniels as her role model.

## *Listing of Works by Gwendoline Butler*

PSEUDONYM: Jennie Melville

---

### INSPECTOR JOHN COFFIN SERIES

*Dead in a Row* . . . . . . . . . . . . . . . . . . . . . . . . . . . . . . . . . .1957
*The Dull Dead* . . . . . . . . . . . . . . . . . . . . . . . . . . . . . . . . . .1958

*The Murdering Kind* . . . . . . . . . . 1958
*Death Lives Next Door*. . . . . . . . . . 1960
(published in the U.S. as *Dine and Be Dead*)
*Make Me a Murderer* . . . . . . . . . . 1961
*Coffin in Oxford*. . . . . . . . . . 1962
*A Coffin for Baby* . . . . . . . . . . 1963
*Coffin Waiting*. . . . . . . . . . 1964
*Coffin in Malta* . . . . . . . . . . 1964
*A Nameless Coffin*. . . . . . . . . . 1966
*Coffin Following* . . . . . . . . . . 1968
*Coffin's Dark Number* . . . . . . . . . . 1969
*A Coffin from the Past*. . . . . . . . . . 1970
*A Coffin for the Canary*. . . . . . . . . . 1974
(published in the U.S. as *Sarsen Place*)
*Coffin on the Water*. . . . . . . . . . 1986
*Coffin in Fashion* . . . . . . . . . . 1987
*Coffin Underground* . . . . . . . . . . 1988
*Coffin in the Black Museum*. . . . . . . . . . 1989
(published in the U.S. as *Coffin in the Museum of Crime*)
*Coffin and the Paper Man* . . . . . . . . . . 1991
*Coffin on Murder Street* . . . . . . . . . . 1992
*A Coffin for Charley* . . . . . . . . . . 1993
*Cracking Open a Coffin*. . . . . . . . . . 1993
*The Coffin Tree* . . . . . . . . . . 1994
*A Dark Coffin* . . . . . . . . . . 1995
*Coffin's Game*. . . . . . . . . . 1999

### Policewoman Charmian Daniels Series (as Jennie Melville)

*Come Home and Be Killed*. . . . . . . . . . 1962
*Burning Is a Substitute for Loving*. . . . . . . . . . 1963
*Murderers' Houses* . . . . . . . . . . 1964
*There Lies Your Love* . . . . . . . . . . 1965
*Nell Alone*. . . . . . . . . . 1966
*A Different Kind of Summer* . . . . . . . . . . 1967
*A New Kind of Killer, An Old Kind of Death* . . . . . . . . . . 1970
(published in the U.S. as *A New Kind of Killer*)
*Murder Has a Pretty Face* . . . . . . . . . . 1981
*Windsor Red* . . . . . . . . . . 1988
*Footsteps in the Blood* . . . . . . . . . . 1990
*Making Good Blood* . . . . . . . . . . 1990
*Witching Murder* . . . . . . . . . . 1990
*Dead Set*. . . . . . . . . . 1992
*Whoever Has the Heart*. . . . . . . . . . 1993
*A Death in the Family* . . . . . . . . . . 1995
*The Morbid Kitchen* . . . . . . . . . . 1996

## Other Crime Novels

*Receipt for Murder* .......... 1956
*The Interloper* .......... 1959
*A Coffin for Pandora* .......... 1973
(also published as *Olivia*)
*The Vesey Inheritance* .......... 1973
*The Brides of Friedberg* .......... 1977
(also published as *Meadowsweet*)
*The Red Staircase* .......... 1980
*Butterfly* .......... 1997

## Other Titles (as Jennie Melville)

*The Hunter in the Shadows* .......... 1969
*The Summer Assassin* .......... 1971
*Ironwood* .......... 1972
*Nun's Castle* .......... 1973
*Raven's Forge* .......... 1975
*Dragon's Eye* .......... 1976
*Axwater* .......... 1978
(also published as *Tarot's Tower*)
*The Wages of Zen* .......... 1979
*The Painted Castle* .......... 1982
*The Hand of Glass* .......... 1983
*Listen to the Children* .......... 1986
*Death in the Garden* .......... 1990
(also published as *Murder in the Garden*)
*A Cure for Dying* .......... 1989
*Baby Drop* .......... 1994

## Novel

*Albion Walk* .......... 1982
(published in England as *Cavalcade*)

(Contributor to anthologies)

# 11
# Patricia Highsmith

This chapter is a departure from the ten previous chapters, in that the subject is the first American to be presented. Of more importance is Tom Ripley, Highsmith's series character. He is not, as might be expected, the chief investigator; instead, he is a criminal, representing the type that must of necessity anticipate how the police will react to a given situation.

Mary Patricia Plangman was born to Jay Bernard and Mary (Coates) Plangman on January 19, 1921, in Fort Worth, Texas. (When it was pointed out to writer Patricia Highsmith that Edgar Allan Poe was also born on January 19, she replied, "I don't believe in astrology. It is also the birthday of Robert E. Lee.") The parents, who were commercial artists, separated before the birth of their daughter, and her maternal grandmother cared for her. At the age of six, Patricia moved with her mother to Greenwich Village, New York. Mrs. Plangman remarried Stanley Highsmith, who adopted Patricia. Her childhood was unhappy, marred by emotional turmoil. She did not meet her biological father until she was 12; she was not close to her mother. Her grandmother, however, she remembered with pleasure.

She learned to read long before she went to school. Later she was enjoying books by Tolstoy and Dostoyevsky. At Julia Richman High School she edited the school newspaper. She graduated from Barnard College in 1942, "being trained for nothing except 'English composition.'" According to journalist Kate Kingsley Skattebol, who knew her at college, Highsmith was a droll, impish wit, who was fond of practical jokes, scatological humor, and bawdy jokes.

Others who knew her later in life remarked on her sense of humor. Patricia edited Barnard's literary magazine, and Skattebol noted that her friend's writing talent was evident then.

The young graduate found a job with a comic book outfit "where at least I learned a trade." A year there, plus Christmas work at Bloomingdale's, brought in just enough money to go to Mexico, where she started a very long book that she never finished.

By 1945, her short story, "The Heroine," was published in *Harper's Bazaar*. It had been rejected by the Barnard College magazine as "too unpleasant."

Her *Strangers on a Train* was published in 1950. Rejected by six publishers, it was accepted after being rewritten. It was a great success, later filmed by Alfred Hitchcock with an altered ending. The background of *Strangers* reflects the environment at mid-century: for instance, the lead characters are traveling by train, not plane; a ceiling fan rather than air conditioning is in use in El Paso: a position is refused by telegram; a child with Down's syndrome is referred to as a Mongolian idiot.

*Strangers* is a psychological study. (Highsmith's family owned a copy of *The Human Mind*, and she studied it constantly.) Charles Bruno, a psychopath, meets Guy Haines, a successful young architect. Bruno hates his father; Guy is angry at his wife. Bruno talks Guy into participating in a scheme whereby Bruno murders Guy's wife and Guy murders Bruno's father. Bruno is convinced that the police will not find the murderers because murderers and victims are strangers to one another. Bruno is obsessed with committing a perfect crime; Guy has a compulsion to confess. (In the Hitchcock movie, only Bruno kills.)

*The Price of Salt* appeared in 1952, written under the pseudonym Claire Morgan. In it Highsmith focused on a lesbian relationship. In time she turned out short stories and nonfiction in addition to novels. Her five-book Ripley series saw publication between the years 1955 and 1995. It was very popular, with two of the books being filmed.

Early in her career, Highsmith was helped by Truman Capote. Later she was friendly with Graham Greene, Gore Vidal and Paul Bowles. Constantly on the move, from 1963 on, she lived in Europe, mainly in England, France and Italy. She finally settled near Locarno, Switzerland. A lover of solitude, she disliked publicity and was known to have walked out on interviews. A strong believer in individual motivation, she contended that drive and ambition count.

Gary Fisketjon, Highsmith's editor at Knopf, remembered her as "a strikingly beautiful woman." Fisketjon also said, "she was not particularly troubled about the fact that she was gay." Duncan Hannah, a New York artist, met her at a book-signing, and described her as almost Buddah-like. "Being under her gaze was like being under a microscope," he reported. A loner who was said to drink and smoke to excess, she loved a cat named Charlotte.

Highsmith's final work was *Small g: A Summer Idyll* (1995) (Gay travel books use the letter "g" to designate a place frequented by both gay and straight.) The book was not received with enthusiasm.

Patricia Highsmith died of leukemia on February 5, 1995, in Locarno, at the age of 74.

In 1957, *The Talented Mr. Ripley* had brought its author the Mystery Writers of America Scroll as well as Le Grand Prix de Littérature Policiere, and seven years later, *The Four Faces of January* had won the Silver Dagger Award. Author Gore Vidal termed her "certainly one of the most interesting writers of this dismal century." She is more widely praised in Europe than in the United States. A French film adaptation of *The Amazing Mr. Ripley (Purple Moon)* was made in 1960. In 1999, an American version was released.

Ripley's career in crime, recounted in five books, keeps the reader turning pages. Tom was always involved in something illegal. At the beginning, it was a scam that involved the Internal Revenue Service. He was an attractive young American with many talents—among them babysitting, accounting, forging signatures, helicopter flying, dice throwing, cooking, impersonating—very strong in the latter. He had few family attachments; his father and mother drowned when he was young and he was raised by an aunt to whom he was not close. Not having a "real" job, he agreed to travel to Italy with all expenses paid. His charge was to persuade Dickie Greenleaf, the son of a rich American, to return home. Tom sailed for Italy, travelers checks in hand.

Tom found the prodigal and his girlfriend. Their way of life appealed to him. The upshot was that he murdered Dickie. Adding weights to the body, he consigned it to a watery grave. Then he impersonated Dickie, who fortunately was the same height and weighed almost the same. Ripley next forged a will that made himself the beneficiary of Dickie's possessions. When Freddie Miles, Dickie's friend, saw through the impersonation, he was quickly disposed of by Ripley.

After the second murder, Ripley tried to assess his behavior from the point of view of the police. He feared that Tenente Roverini in Rome might get suspicious. But he decided that he was safe for the time being if he continued to do and say the right thing. But was he going to see policemen waiting for him in Alexandria? Istanbul? Bombay? Rio? No good thinking about it, he told himself.

He married Heloise Plissot, the daughter of a wealthy businessman. Heloise might have been suspicious, but did not know about her husband's criminal activities. They owned a villa named Belle Ombre just outside Paris. Ripley (and his wife also) enjoyed travel to exotic places, but was always happy to return home. The couple had no children. Tom was interested in gardening, music and art; he built a greenhouse, bought a harpsichord and collected paintings, original and forged. It was clear that he was leading the good life, and there were endless references to eating gourmet foods and drinking fine wines.

He was making his living as a silent partner in the Buckminster Gallery in London, which dealt in forgeries of an artist named Derwatt. Derwatt had committed suicide, but art patrons were led to believe that he was living in Mexico as a recluse. Keeping the forgery business above suspicion was not easy; it motivated Tom to commit additional murders and unbecoming acts. When his victims were evil—for instance, members of the Mafia—Tom was able to convince himself that murdering them was justifiable. But despite persuading himself that his conscience was clear, he had uneasy memories of an English police inspector and also one in Nemours. However, in the last book of the series, Tom was free, and there was no hint that the police had any important evidence against him.

Critics have delved deeply into Ripley's psychology and of course the fact that he escaped justice. From interviews with Highsmith, there is some information about her ideas when she created the Tom Ripley books.

"I think of the story first," she said, "I think of the events. Is it interesting or is it amusing or is it unexpected or is it almost unbelievable?" She also admitted that she would much rather entertain than moralize. And she thought "that to mock lip-service morality and to have a character amoral, such as Ripley, is entertaining." It was her stated belief that there were plenty walking around the streets of Chicago and Marseilles "who have killed somebody and sleep well." She also admitted to having less interest in style than in emotion.

Highsmith noted a close psychological resemblance between Tom and Bruno of *Strangers,* whom she designated a psychopath.

"I couldn't write about peasants," she declared. "I have to write, any writer has to write, about the class of people that he knows." To illustrate her point, she cited an experience she had as a teenager. She tried to write a story about an Italian family. Although she had many Italian classmates, she found herself unable to do it, "because I had never lived in their households with 10 or 11 people sitting at the dining room table." So Ripley was middle class, as was his creator.

According to Highsmith, "I couldn't make an interesting story out of a moron." So Ripley was reasonably intelligent—enough to have had some worries about the outcome of his outrageous exploits.

She was interested in guilt. Although Ripley managed to rationalize most of his crimes, he did feel guilty about murdering Dickie.

However unconventional, the Ripley books remain popular. Perhaps Highsmith died before she fulfilled her plans for Tom. Perhaps not.

She said she thought, "Why shouldn't I write about a few characters who also go free?" Why not, indeed? It makes interesting reading—just what she intended.

## *Listing of Works by (Mary) Patricia Highsmith*

PSEUDONYM: Claire Morgan

### TOM RIPLEY SERIES

*The Talented Mr. Ripley** . . . . . . . . . . 1955
*Ripley under Ground** . . . . . . . . . . 1970
*Ripley's Game** . . . . . . . . . . 1974
*The Boy Who Followed Ripley* . . . . . . . . . . 1980
*Ripley under Water* . . . . . . . . . . 1992

*These titles are collected as *The Mysterious Mr. Ripley* . . . . . . . . . . 1985

### NOVEL (AS CLAIRE MORGAN)

*The Price of Salt* . . . . . . . . . . 1952
(reprinted as *Carol* under author's name with a new author's afterword, 1984, 1990 [London])

### OTHER CRIME NOVELS

*Strangers on a Train* . . . . . . . . . . 1950
*The Blunderer* . . . . . . . . . . 1954
(published in the U.S. also as *Lament for a Lover, 1956*)
*Deep Water* . . . . . . . . . . 1957
*A Game for the Living* . . . . . . . . . . 1958
*This Sweet Sickness* . . . . . . . . . . 1960
*The Cry of the Owl* . . . . . . . . . . 1962
*The Glass Cell* . . . . . . . . . . 1964
*The Two Faces of January* . . . . . . . . . . 1964
*The Story-Teller* . . . . . . . . . . 1965
*Those Who Walk Away* . . . . . . . . . . 1967
*The Tremor of Forgery* . . . . . . . . . . 1969
*A Dog's Ransom* . . . . . . . . . . 1972
*Edith's Diary* . . . . . . . . . . 1977
*People Who Knock on the Door* . . . . . . . . . . 1983
*Found in the Street* . . . . . . . . . . 1986
*Small g: A Summer Idyll* . . . . . . . . . . 1995

## SHORT STORIES

*The Snail-Watcher and Other Stories* . . . . . . . . . . . . . . . . . . . . . . . . . . . . . .1970
(published in England as *Eleven*)
*Kleine Geschichten für Weiberfeinde* . . . . . . . . . . . . . . . . . . . . . . . . . . . . . . . .1974
(published in the U.S. and England as *Little Tales of Misogny)*
*The Animal-Lover's Book of Beastly Murder* . . . . . . . . . . . . . . . . . . . . . . . . . .1975
*Slowly, Slowly in the Wind* . . . . . . . . . . . . . . . . . . . . . . . . . . . . . . . . . . . . . . .1979
*The Black House* . . . . . . . . . . . . . . . . . . . . . . . . . . . . . . . . . . . . . . . . . . . . .1981
*Mermaids on the Golf Course and Other Stories* . . . . . . . . . . . . . . . . . . . . . . .1985
*Tales of Natural and Unnatural Catastrophes* . . . . . . . . . . . . . . . . . . . . . . . . .1987

## JUVENILE

(with Doris Sanders) *Miranda the Panda Is on the Veranda* . . . . . . . . . . . . .1958

## NONFICTION

*Plotting and Writing Suspense Fiction* . . . . . . . . . . . . . . . . . . . . . . . . . . . . .1966

# 12

# Carolyn G. Heilbrun
## *(Amanda Cross)*

Carolyn G. Heilbrun might be called the Dorothy L. Sayers of American women mystery writers in that both shower the reader with scholarly quotes. In a more serious vein, Heilbrun, who had great regard for Sayers, is primarily an educator who effectively uses the detective story to reinforce her message.

Carolyn Gold was born in East Orange, New Jersey, to Archibald and Estelle (Roemer) Gold on January 13, 1926. She was their only child. Later in life, Carolyn admitted great admiration for her father, an accountant and business consultant who became a millionaire after experiencing extreme poverty. She had a sense of protectiveness towards her mother, who "never had the courage to do anything herself in life." According to Carolyn, Estelle Gold stayed at home, was bored and knew that her life was a loss. In view of this, she advised her daughter to be independent, and Carolyn was influenced by her mother's message.

Archibald observed the Jewish High Holidays, but his wife was opposed to Judaism. As a child of humanistic Jews, the future professor grew up in Central Park West in Manhattan, attended summer camps (and hated swimming), spent two summers at ranches, and had an expensive education. She became a reader early in life; she liked the Nancy Drew and Judy Bolton mysteries at first, then turned to the novels of Virginia Woolf and Willa Cather. At a branch of the New York Public Library she worked her way through the biographical section in alphabetical order, noticing that there were few biographies of women. This was the beginning of her long fascination with biography. Her father insisted that she learn to touch type. Later she learned word processing.

She entered Wellesley College, was elected to Phi Beta Kappa, and graduated in 1947, majoring in literature and philosophy. She has said she disliked Wellesley and its ladylike WASP Republican students who seemed to think of nothing except getting engaged. (With regard to being ladylike, she has made it clear that in the 1960s, she greatly welcomed the new freedom of being able to wear non-feminine clothes.) She also found Wellesley "in the nicest way, anti-Semitic." She has not been critical of the quality of education provided by her alma mater.

In 1945, Carolyn, at 19, married James Heilbrun, a future professor of economics. He was then a Harvard student, recently drafted, and about to be assigned to the Pacific Theater. She at one time tried to conceal from young people her wartime marriage because she believed it set a poor example. James Heilbrun is still her husband, and she has referred to her marriage of more than 50 years as "probably the single most fortunate factor on my life."

She refused to accept what was then the expected destiny for a woman—only to marry and have children. Her goal was the Ph.D. and to have a profession; she was an intellectual with a love of literature. She did a short stint in radio and publicity before graduate school. In 1951, she received the Master of Arts from Columbia University and eight years later, the doctorate.

After serving as an instructor at Brooklyn College in 1960, Heilbrun began her teaching career at Columbia University, focusing on feminist issues often related to literature. For this she has been recognized with honorary degrees and other awards. She has been a member and president of the executive council of the Modern Languages Association. She has also served as visiting lecturer at Yale University, Swathmore College and Union Theological Seminary and as visiting professor at Princeton University and at the University of California at Santa Cruz.

The year 1963 saw Professor Heilbrun the mother of three children, the oldest less than eight years old; she had a new large dog; her husband was studying for the Ph.D. Stressful as the situation might be, she was leading a full and satisfying life. Nevertheless, she wanted to write a detective novel and in the process create an individual whose destiny offered more possibility than Heilbrun could imagine for herself—someone, for example, free of domestic chores. She has said that at the time, she could not find any detective fiction that she enjoyed reading.

The character that she constructed was Kate Fansler whose exploits were featured in a series, the first book of which was published in 1964. That book—*In the Last Analysis*—won a Scroll from the Mystery

Writers of America. Various titles have been translated into Japanese, French, German, Spanish, Italian, Swedish, and Finnish.

According to Heilbrun:

> My sort of detective fiction will always be accused of snobbery. This, I have decided, is inevitable. I myself am that apparently rare anomaly, an individual who likes courtesy and intelligence, but would like to see the end of reaction, stereotyped sex-roles, and convention that arises from the fear of change, and the anxiety change brings. I loathe violence, and do not consider sex a spectator sport, I like humor, but fear unkindness, and the cruelty of power.

The Fansler series is written under the pseudonym of Amanda Cross. Heilbrun believed that when it came to granting tenure, authorities at the university would turn her down if she were known as the author of detective stories. She based this assumption of the fact that a male colleague who wrote mysteries had been denied tenure. (The Kate Fansler mystery entitled *The James Joyce Murder* noted prejudice against mysteries among academics.) Heilbrun later wrote that the secrecy of her pen name gave her a sense of control over her own life in those pretenure, prewomen's movement days. The identity of Amanda Cross was kept secret for six years. Heilbrun became a full professor with tenure in 1972.

She has also enjoyed success in her scholastic writing career. For example, *Writing a Woman's Life* was a best seller. She had wanted to write Dorothy L. Sayers' biography, but the Sayers executors chose James Brabazon. Heilbrun did, however, write an authorized biography of Gloria Steinem.

According to Boke, because of Heilbrun's increasingly high profile in feminist studies, women's institutes around the country vied for her support, and she was appointed to the most elite groups formed around women's issues. One of these groups includes the University of Michigan Series on Women and Culture, which is devoted to publishing books on various aspects of feminism. Heilbrun was elected to its advisory board in 1977.

After 32 years at Columbia, she took early retirement at 66 rather than 70. She claims that throughout that period, her male colleagues ignored her and left her isolated. The Heilbruns have an apartment in New York City, but in summer, enjoy their second home in the Berkshire Hills in Massachusetts. She continues to read Sara Paretsky, Sue Grafton, John le Carré, Michael Gilbert, Dick Francis and Tony Hillerman. She admits to being a fan of email.

While in her 60s, Heilbrun was asked if her father would have been so supportive had she had a brother. She concluded that a brother would have pushed her into a stereotypical female role; she would have been educated, but not expected to insist upon a professional career or to have revolutionary opinions.

She considers the most important achievement of her career the discovery of the friendships of women. According to her book, *The Last Gift of Time: Life Beyond Sixty*, she now finds it reassuring to think of life as borrowed time—with the chance to live or die; each day she chooses life because it is a choice.

Kate Fansler is a witty amateur detective who depends largely on her literary skills to solve mysteries, A professor of Victorian literature, she often takes on cases that involve academics.

Kate was born to wealth and position—governess, private school and so on. She has three older brothers, for whom she does not care. They conveniently supply nieces and nephews when needed. Her parents are dead. At the beginning of the series, this passionate feminist loves her independence and her work too much to desire marriage.

The professor is beautiful—tall and thin. She likes to drink and she smokes*; she eats plain food and thick soup; she refers to God as "She"; she dislikes television and football; she does not jog; she likes solitude; she enjoys John le Carré; she believes in fate, or destiny; and she has a morbid fascination with institutions, the army, the church, the prestigious universities because they are so implacable, she ages as the series progresses; in *The Question of Max* (1970) she is described as middle-aged. British author Antonia Fraser has noted, "Cross, in allowing Fansler her own logical development from 1964, has managed to chronicle the history of women during the key period in the most accessible way as well as to provide values of literate, witty entertainment." Heilbrun has said that she regrets making Fansler beautiful.

The man in Kate's life is Reed Amhearst, who, when first presented, is an assistant district attorney. (Later he becomes a professor of law.) Distinguishing between convention and morality, Fansler after a while is willing to have a sexual relationship with him and to acknowledge it openly. She marries Reed in *Poetic Justice* (1970). She considers her marriage more the setting than the immediate concern of her life; she wears no ring; she does not use Reed's surname; she does not depend on him financially; and she does not want children.The marriage is a good one, surviving the fact that Reed is not familiar with James Joyce and, no doubt, other such authors so important to the wife of a professor of English.

**In 1988, Heilbrun wrote that Kate Fansler has stuck to her martinis and cigarettes as a sort of camouflage for her more revolutionary opinions and activities.*

Besides being skilled in literary and psychological analysis, Kate is involved in issues of the day, particularly those related to women's rights. To illustrate, *Poetic Justice* shows her involvement in keeping strong at her university a college for dropouts who have become more mature and for older women seeking to be something other than housewives; *The Theban Mysteries* (1972) is concerned with intergenerational conflict, especially the Vietnam War. *The Imperfect Spy* (1995) addresses the battered woman syndrome.

Kate does not particularly like travel. However, she goes where she has to—to London and Geneva, as in *The Players Come Again*. She travels around the country, spending time on campuses other than her own—*Death in a Tenured Position* is set at Harvard, where patriarchal pressures drive a female professor to suicide. Dean and Kate own a cabin in a secluded area of the Berkshire Hills, and she enjoys being able to go there alone.

The reader can never forget that Fansler is a feminist—for example, with regard to a proposed biography of a woman married to a famous author, Kate tells herself, "However good Max may be, a woman ought to write that biography." She admits that to be a thoroughly sexist remark. And the reader is constantly reminded that Fansler has a background in literature. *Poetic Justice* has numerous references to Auden; *The Theban Mysteries* contains allusions to *Antigone*; Kipling is prominent in *A Trap for Fools*; a poem by Herbert is pivotal in *Death in a Tenured Position*—and so on.

How Fansler interacts with Butler illustrates the author's skill in presenting an interesting minor character and at the same time adding to the reader's understanding of the main character.

As second in command of the university's security department, Butler can supply crucial information about who had access to Levy Hall when a professor fell out, jumped out, or was pushed out his office window seven stories from the ground.

Butler had emigrated from Ireland 20 years previously. He cannot see that murder is so much worse than what is currently happening on campus—homosexuality (for which AIDS is God's righteous punishment), fornication, drugs, and disruption, all what he calls mortal sins. He complains that he cannot pick up a black because that might be an infringement on civil rights, even if Butler thinks the man is intent on rape, mayhem or burglary.

It is clear that Butler is narrow minded and rigid. Obviously his conservative opinions are in conflict with Fansler's liberal thinking. But he does not criticize her feminist views, though he lets her know that his wife took his name, wears his ring and is supported by him. But his racist views do not dictate his actions. As Kate works with him, she becomes increasingly fond of him. He respects the rules they were playing by. And he knows from memory much poetry, particularly Houseman. Perhaps this mutual interest helped to neutralize each's opinion of the other, creating a good working relationship.

Heilbrun writes that she invented Kate Fansler at first as a fantasy figure, then as Heilbrun herself aged, her creation became more realistic. She gave Kate parents, already dead, whom their daughter could dislike, in spite of the comfortable income they had left her. According to Heilbrun, through Fansler, she could write in a popular medium, the destiny she hoped for women. It is her desire that younger women will imitate the professor/sleuth, not in smoking and drinking, not necessarily in marrying or declining to have children, but instead, in daring to use her security in order to be brave on behalf of other women, and to discover new stories for women.

## *Listing of Works by Carolyn G. Heilbrun*

PSEUDONYM: Amanda Cross

### PROFESSOR KATE FANSLER SERIES (AS AMANDA CROSS)

*In the Last Analysis* .......... 1964
*The James Joyce Murder* .......... 1967
*Poetic Justice* .......... 1970
*The Theban Mysteries* .......... 1972
*The Question of Max* .......... 1976
*Death in a Tenured Position* .......... 1981
*Sweet Death, Kind Death* .......... 1984
*No Word from Winifred* .......... 1986
*A Trap for Fools* .......... 1989
*The Players Come Again* .......... 1990
*An Imperfect Spy* .......... 1995
*The Puzzled Heart* .......... 1998

### OTHER WORKS

*The Garnett Family* .......... 1961
*Christopher Isherwood* .......... 1970
*Towards a Recognition of Androgyny: Aspects of Male and Female in Literature* .......... 1973
(published in England as *Towards Androgyny*)
*Reinventing Womanhood* .......... 1979

*Writing a Woman's Life* . . . . . . . . . . . . . . . . . . . . . . . . . . . . . . . . . . . . . . . .1988
*Hamlet's Mother and Other Women* . . . . . . . . . . . . . . . . . . . . . . . . . . . . . . . .1990
*The Education of a Woman: The Life of Gloria Steinem* . . . . . . . . . . . . . . . . .1995
*The Last Gift of Time: Life Beyond Sixty* . . . . . . . . . . . . . . . . . . . . . . . . . . .1997
(editor) *Lady Ottoline's Album* . . . . . . . . . . . . . . . . . . . . . . . . . . . . . . . . . . . .1976
(editor) with Margaret R. Higonnet *The Representation of Women in Fiction* . . . . . . . . . . . . . . . . . . . . . . . . . . . . . . . . . . . . . . . . . . . . . . .1983

(Contributor to nonfiction works)

# 13
# Ruth Rendell

A critic once wrote that it was infuriating to see Ruth Rendell consistently referred to as the new Agatha Christie. Infuriating because, in that writer's opinion, Rendell is incomparably better, attempting more and achieving more. At the least, Rendell is one of England's most popular mystery writers.

Ruth Barbara Grasemann was born in London on February 17, 1930, to Arthur and Elba (Kruse) Grasemann, both teachers. She was their only child. According to what she said in an interview in 1988, the Grasemanns had an unhappy marriage, and this cast a shadow on Ruth's childhood. The Swedish born Mrs. Grasemann found it difficult to pronounce Ruth, so she called her daughter Barbara—as did most relatives and close friends. As a child, having two names gave young Ruth a sense that she was somehow out of place. Elba Grasemann suffered from multiple sclerosis.

Ruth grew up in suburban East London, where her father built a modern-style house for his family. To Arthur Grasemann she owes her love of houses—a love evidenced in her writing. She remembers sitting on her father's knee while he read aloud Hardy. (She had so much Hardy via that route that for many years she had no desire to read that author.) She graduated in 1948 from the Loughton Country High School in Essex. Since she appears to have been almost a loner, it is not surprising that she began to write fiction at an early age. At 15, she had completed a novel written in verse.

From 1948 to 1952, Ruth worked on the staff of some small local newspapers. In 1950, she married Donald Rendell, a journalist with the *Chigwell Times*. She resigned to take care of their son, whom they had named Simon.

Fiction writing was more to Rendell's liking than journalism, but for some time, publication of her short stories eluded her. When she submitted a novel to Hutchinson, a British publisher, she was informed that it would require rewriting. She was also asked if she had anything else. She did have on hand a detective novel, *From Doon with Death,* that she had written "really for fun." She made rapid revisions and submitted it. Hutchinson accepted the manuscript, and very soon Doubleday bought the America rights.

Years later Rendell told an interviewer, "Having now established for myself a means of livelihood, I was constrained to work within the detective genre and doing so I found that I preferred to deal with the psychological, emotional aspects of human nature...."

Rendell has been very productive, writing traditional detective stories in the Wexford series, and non-series crime novels with a strong psychological atmosphere as well as short stories. In 1986, she began to use the pseudonym Barbara Vine for some books whose characters are, according to her, "ordinary people under extraordinary pressure." This is to distinguish them from the other non-series books that deal with psychopaths. Barbara, of course, is one of her given names, while Vine is the maiden name of her paternal great-grandmother. Thus, Rendell makes it clear that she writes three rather different types of books

A reader, she finishes as many as five books a week. The fields are diverse; for instance, she is interested in Freud, Jung, and Adler; and she is an authority on the Oxford Movement. Her favorite play is *Antony and Cleopatra;* she admires Patricia Highsmith; her favorite novel is *The Way of All Flesh* by Samuel Butler; she considers *Crime and Punishment* one of the world's greatest novels; every year she rereads Ford Madox Ford's *The Good Soldier* for "its structure [and] its author's skill in dealing with time." Quotes from non-mystery writers frequently appear in her works, but she does not indulge in this as frequently as Amanda Cross.

This British author places great importance on characterization. She says that she sometimes thinks herself into a character. Also, looking at portraits in a photograph album or at an art gallery helps her to describe a character. Sometimes her dialogue is based on the conversation of strangers. She admits: "I listen in pubs to people talking and in restaurants and at airports, in trains, in shops. And when I write down what they say, I repeat it in my head, listening with that inner ear for the right cadence, the ring of authenticity." She once said:

> The development of a human personality is what I'm really interested in. I like to work on characters. I want to know what will become of

> them. ... I think people can be driven to commit murder, and I'm interested in the pressures that are put on people and the stresses that they suffer from other people.

Writing—and that includes publicity—is very much a part of Rendell's life—so much so, that she has little time for other things. She calls herself a compulsive writer—producing too many books and sometimes writing too much; she also does extensive rewriting. But, she has ideas—and wants to see them put into print. Rendell concedes that she is not a great writer; she sees herself, rather, as an entertainer.

Her honors are many, including two Edgar Allan Poe Awards for short stories and three Gold Dagger Awards for novels. In 1992, the British Crime Writers Association, sponsored by Cartier, conferred on her the Diamond Dagger Award. (Among other recipients are P.D. James and John Le Carré.) According to *Current Biography Yearbook*, the Wexford novels have generally failed to charm critics as much as they have readers. Some have been adapted for British television and later aired in the United States.

Rendell and her husband were divorced in 1975, then remarried in 1977. She is a vegetarian; she also has long been involved in antinuclear and antivivisectionist activities. Her son, a sociologist, lives in the United States, and she has paid him frequent visits. On retiring in the 1980s, her husband became a dendrologist. The couple also moved from London to Suffolk, where they have a 12th century cottage on 11 acres of woodland. Rendell's 1989 book entitled *Ruth Rendell's Suffolk* expresses her fascination with the area and is illustrated with exquisite photographs.

Diana-Cooper Clark once asked Rendell about similarities between Rendell's writing and that of Christie. Rendell replied:

> Although she had some wonderful plots, marvelous ideas, I don't think she ever bothered to go into her characters in depth. I don't think she ever studied the time that she was living in, and her novels are peopled with a group of stock characters. ... That is why I say she was superficial, and I don't think that I am. I wish that I could think of her plots and her wonderful surprises, and I think in that she was vastly superior to me, but I don't think she was my equal in characterization and emotional content.

The Wexford series began with *From Doon with Death* in 1964 and apparently will continue, although Rendell prefers to write her non-series works. She has said she plans to kill off her Chief Inspector in a book to be published after her death. Presumably the public still enjoys Wexford and his cohorts.

Most of the action is related to the fictional Home Counties town of Kingsmarkham in Sussex. It is there that Reginald Wexford fights crime—and finds plenty to keep him busy. (Rendell told an interviewer, "I don't want people to see Kingsmarkham as a pretty village.")

Wexford was first presented in *Doon* as: "Tall, thick-set without being fat, 52 years old, the very prototype of an actor playing a top-brass policeman." He has since suffered from hypertension and at one point had a stroke. Devoted to his work, he shows intelligence, intuition and imagination; he is unusually tolerant and understanding. These qualities make him a respected and talented local personage. He loves Dora, his wife. Their adult daughters are Sylvia, married and a mother of two, and Sheila, an actress, Naturally he has faults: pride, for one thing, and he is known at times to have sexual temptations. His creator says he is an amalgam of classic detectives, Georges Simenon's Maigrait in particular. Wexford reads widely and uses quotes from literature. Rendell likes to write about him "because he is me and he is my father." She notes that both she and her creation "have our heads in the clouds and our feet on the ground."

One of Wexford's most reliable colleagues is Mike Burden. The two men work well together and their frequent discussions about their cases often prove fruitful. At times, Burden's personal life becomes almost as important as Wexford's, adding variety to the plot. In *No More Dying*, the deputy is disconsolate after the death of his wife. At one point, he thinks he wants to marry a woman whose son has disappeared. The son is found, an old murder is solved and later, but not in that book, Burden marries someone else.

After Rendell visited China, Wexford does, too, in *The Speaker of Mandarin.* He ends up investigating the death of a member of his tour group. He attends a rock festival in *Some Live and Some Die.* The settings of the books tend to be contemporary rather than timeless. This is brought out in *Road Rage,* which deals with the environmental issue.

With regard to being contemporary, Rendell was asked in 1981 why she had not used a female police inspector in her series. She answered that in the early 1960s, when Wexford was created, things were not as they were some 20 years later. At the time Wesford was introduced, men were the people and women the others. According to her, had her chief character come into existence in the 1980s, she would probably have chosen a woman.

In 1997, *Road Rage*, an Inspector Wexford Mystery, won the Grand Master Award of the Mystery Writers of America. Some glimpses into that book reflect Rendell's literary skill and show why she was a recipient of the award.

Dora Wexford has joined the committee of the newly formed KABAL, Kingsmarkham Against the Bypass and Landfill. Her husband is against the new bypass, but he is not fighting it. He asks himself if he would give up his car for England. He decides he wants to eat his cake and have it, too. Burden favors the bypass because he thinks it will ease traffic congestion; also, he thinks of the old days when there was no fuss about such matters—people abided by government decisions.

The Wexfords are about to have another grandchild. Sheila is the mother and the father her actor friend. They are not married, but this is the 1960s, and they regard it as a joyous event.

When news about the bypass got out, things began to happen in Kingsmarkham. The town was being visited by representatives of environmental groups and also by various individuals. One of these was a woman clad in a sandwich board with a message, under which she was naked. Tree fellers moved in in droves to build themselves abodes of planks and tarpaulins on the tops of oaks and ashes. The means of approach was by ladders that could be pulled up after the occupant entered his home. Wexford tells Dora that this is just the beginning—there will be hordes of security guards installed to protect the contractors.

When a dense mass of brambles is cut away, the badly decomposed body of a young girl is found. She is quickly identified as Ulrike Ranke, a German student who was visiting England for Easter. She had been raped and strangled, and gone was £500 she had carried on her in notes. A search of the pockets of her jeans recovers 25 amphetamine tablets and a packet of cannabis

At the time of her disappearance earlier, Wexford and Burden were involved in the interrogation. A photo had been produced that showed Ulrike wearing a string of pearls. Her parents said that on her 18th birthday, they had given her a string of matched cultured pearls worth the equivalent of £13,000. The pearls, too, were not to be found.

To Burden, the prime suspect was Stanley Trotter of Contemporary cars who had answered a taxi call from the murdered girl the evening of her death, but he claimed he never picked her up. He had a criminal record; and among his belongings had been found a string of artificial pearls.

There was nothing against Trotter, and lacking such proof, Burden had to let him go, although he was absolutely convinced that he had his man. Wexford was not so sure.

With Kingsmarkham invaded by bypass demonstrators from London and even masked raiders, it becomes apparent that five of its citizens are gone missing. One of them is Dora Wexford. Intending to take the train to London to visit her new granddaughter, she had called Contemporary Cars to send a taxi to get her to Kingsmartin Station. She had not arrived there.

A message from a group calling itself Sacred Globe reveals that the five gone missing are being held as hostages. The price to save them will be revealed later. All national newspapers and the Kingsmartin Police are to be informed. Sacred Globe describes itself as saving the earth from destruction by all means in its power. A second message announces that the price is to stop the bypass. If the price is not paid, the hostages will die one by one.

Suspense builds as Wexford and his staff, which includes women, race against time to identify Sacred Globe and find the whereabouts of the hostages. And in the process, Ulrike Ranke's murderer is found and arrested.

Wexford and Burden being men police officers not withstanding, *Road Rage* holds the reader's interest and stimulates thinking about various aspects of the environmental issue.

## *Listing of Works by Ruth Rendell*

PSEUDONYM: Barbara Vine

---

INSPECTOR WEXFORD SERIES

*From Doon with Death* . . . . . . . . . . . . . . . . . . . . . . . . . . . . . . .1964
*A New Lease on Death* . . . . . . . . . . . . . . . . . . . . . . . . . . . . . . .1967
(published also as *Sins of the Fathers)*
*A Wolf to the Slaughter* . . . . . . . . . . . . . . . . . . . . . . . . . . . . . .1967
*The Best Man to Die* . . . . . . . . . . . . . . . . . . . . . . . . . . . . . . .1969
*A Guilty Thing Surprised* . . . . . . . . . . . . . . . . . . . . . . . . . . . . .1970
*No More Dying Then* . . . . . . . . . . . . . . . . . . . . . . . . . . . . . . .1971
*Murder Being Once Done* . . . . . . . . . . . . . . . . . . . . . . . . . . . . .1972
*Some Lie and Some Die* . . . . . . . . . . . . . . . . . . . . . . . . . . . . . .1973
*Shake Hands Forever* . . . . . . . . . . . . . . . . . . . . . . . . . . . . . . .1975
*A Sleeping Life* . . . . . . . . . . . . . . . . . . . . . . . . . . . . . . . . . .1978
*Put on by Cunning* . . . . . . . . . . . . . . . . . . . . . . . . . . . . . . . .1981
(published in the U.S. as *Death Notes*)
*The Speaker of Mandarin* . . . . . . . . . . . . . . . . . . . . . . . . . . . . .1983
*An Unkindness of Ravens* . . . . . . . . . . . . . . . . . . . . . . . . . . . . .1985
*The Veiled One* . . . . . . . . . . . . . . . . . . . . . . . . . . . . . . . . . .1988
*Kissing the Gunner's Daughter* . . . . . . . . . . . . . . . . . . . . . . . . . .1993
*Simisola* . . . . . . . . . . . . . . . . . . . . . . . . . . . . . . . . . . . . .1994
*Road Rage* . . . . . . . . . . . . . . . . . . . . . . . . . . . . . . . . . . . .1997

## Other Crime Novels

*To Fear a Painted Lady* .... 1965
*Vanity Dies Hard* .... 1965
(also published as *In Sickness and in Health*)
*The Secret House of Death* .... 1968
*One Across, Two Down* .... 1971
*The Face of Trespass* .... 1974
*A Demon in My View* .... 1976
*A Judgement in Stone* .... 1977
*Make Death Love Me* .... 1979
*The Lake of Darkness* .... 1980
*Master of the Moor* .... 1982
*The Killing Doll* .... 1984
*The Tree of Hands* .... 1984
*Live Flesh* .... 1986
*A Warning to the Curious* .... 1987
*Heartstones* .... 1987
*Talking to Strange Men* .... 1987
*The Veiled One* .... 1988
*The Bridesmaid* .... 1989
*Going Wrong* .... 1990
*The Crocodile Bird* .... 1993
*A Sight for Sore Eyes* .... 1999

## Single Novels (as Barbara Vine)

*The Dark-Adapted Eye* .... 1986
*A Fatal Inversion* .... 1987
*The House of Stairs* .... 1989
*Gallowglass* .... 1990
*King Solomon's Carpet* .... 1991
*Asta's Book* .... 1993
*Anna's Book* .... 1993
*No Night is Too Long* .... 1994
*The Brimstone Wedding* .... 1996

## Short Story Collections

*The Fallen Curtain and Other Stories* .... 1976
*Means of Evil and Other Stories* .... 1979
*The Fever Tree and Other Stories* .... 1982
*The New Girl Friend* .... 1985
*Collected Short Stories* .... 1987
*The Copper Peacock, and Other Stories* .... 1991
*Blood Lines: Long and Short Stories* .... 1995

## Other Publications

*Ruth Rendell's Suffolk* (photographs by Paul Bowden) . . . . . . . . . . . . . . . . .1989
(editor) *A Warning to the Curious: The Ghost Stories of M.R. James* . . . . . . .1987
(editor, with Colin Ward) *Undermining the Central Line* . . . . . . . . . . . . .1989

# 14
# Edna Buchanan

This author distinguished herself by winning a Pulitzer Prize in journalism. Her experiences and skill in crime reporting make her detective fiction authentic and vivid.

Edna Rydzik Buchanan was born near Paterson, New Jersey. There seems to be some doubt about the date of her birth, but March 16, 1939, appears in one source. Her maternal ancestors were French Huguenots who came to this continent many generations ago. Her mother, who eloped with the son of a Polish factory worker, was born in Ukraine.

The young Edna was read to by her mother. When the mother was busy, the child would wander about the neighborhood looking for someone to read to her. Her grandmother, who lived two doors away, loved her, but could not grant her request because that relative could not speak English.

By the age of six, Edna was looking over the tabloid-size New York *Daily News* with its numerous photos and easy-to-read headlines. She was particularly fond of the Sunday issue, which featured a crime case—often a murder. By the time she was seven, this youngster had finished the Ellery Queen books (also *Forever Amber*), and had on hand many copies of *Reader's Digest* and *The Saturday Evening Post*.

At that time, the Rydziks invested everything they had in a small neighborhood tavern in a nearby blue-collar community named Singac. Her father was frequently involved in gambling, drinking and philandering.

Mrs. Rydzik decided to leave him. A judge ordered him to pay child support for Edna and her sister, three years younger, but nothing was ever paid. He left town and was never heard of again by members of his family.

**Edna Buchanan by Jim Virga. By courtesy of Hyperion.**

The Rydziks moved frequently. School—wherever it was—was an ordeal for Edna, who did poorly in math and physical education. Stories, which she read, wrote and daydreamed, provided an escape.

There was one bit of cheer in her life. Her seventh-grade teacher, Edna Mae Tunis, said to her, in the presence of her classmates, "Promise me you will dedicate a book to me someday."

It would be 1987 when this happened, but the words provided great encouragement to the young student. Mrs. Tunis died before Edna went to high school; she lived long enough to see Edna's first rejection slip. It was from *The Saturday Evening Post* and a sign that she was serious about becoming a writer. And through Edna's writing, the teacher's daughter was located many years later—and found to be following her mother's profession.

To support the family, Mrs. Rydzik had three jobs—one at a coat factory full time, one at a candle factory full time; on weekends she was a waitress. At 12, Edna had a summer job in the coat factory where her mother worked, and sometimes she substituted for Mrs. Rydzik on the midnight shift at the candle factory, sometimes on the all-night shift as a waitress. By the time she was 16, she was working behind the sock counter at W.F. Woolworth's. Other part-time jobs included a stint at the baby clothes department at W.T. Grant's, at a photo studio, at a mail-order house, and at a dry cleaning shop.

Full-time work at Western Electric finally provided mother and daughter some security. The former was able to give up a second job, while the latter, having finished high school, could work full time. College was out of the question because of their financial situation. However, she was now able to buy a car, a Nash Metropolitan convertible. She also enrolled in a night course in creative writing. The instructor compared a suspense story that she wrote to the early work of Tennessee Williams.

The work at Western Electric was hardly stimulating although Edna had been transferred from switchboard wiring to office work in the same plant. One summer, when it shut down for two weeks, she and her mother took their first vacation—on the Jersey shore. It rained every day of the week they were there, prompting them to set their sites on Florida for a future vacation.

They visited Miami Beach in July, 1961. Edna fell in love with the area and promptly moved there. No job presented itself, but she did enroll in a creative writing class. Through a member of the class (whom she would marry), she learned of an opening in the Miami Beach *Daily Sun*, a tabloid with a circulation of only 10,000.

Her boss was Maude Massengale, the society editor. Massengale taught her how to cover functions, how to write headlines, layout, and other fundamentals. On occasion, the newcomer was permitted to write Maude's column and sometimes even Letters to the Editor. Such letters were signed with fictitious names, the aim being to spur interest in various issues on the part of non-employee readers. Rydzik recalled the period as the dying days of old-time newspapers, the days of linotype machines, hot type and metal engraving. She received less than the minimum wage; overtime did not exist. On the other hand, she was gaining experience.

The student from the writing class was John Buchanan, a reporter for the *Daily Sun*. He and Edna were married for a brief period, then divorced in 1965. Unlike her father, he was always there. If that had been the attraction, it was not sufficient to hold them together.

Buchanan had left the *Sun* and needed work. On trying *The Miami Herald*, the South's best and largest newspaper, she was told not to apply unless she had a degree in journalism or five years' experience. The *Sun* was under new management, and its new editor, Ted Crail, welcomed the fact that she would not have to unlearn anything. However, the publisher considered a divorcee "unstable and unreliable," and she was not hired.

To support herself Buchanan did freelance writing for trade journals. Since she was paid for writing by the inch, she was as wordy as possible. When the publisher of the *Sun* left, the paper's editor hired her—this time to report hard news—also to shoot suitable pictures.

The new situation gave her valuable on-the-job-training. Sometimes people went out of their way to cooperate—Mayor Chuck Hill, for example. After a storm had caused his new boat to sink, workers pumped for hours to resurface it, Buchanan arrived too late to get an underwater photograph. To make that possible, the mayor ordered his hired workers to sink the boat by refilling it. When Buchanan voiced concern that photographing under such conditions might be unethical, the mayor assured her that they were only recreating the scene.

Buchanan married a second time. Her husband was Emmett Miller, a police officer. They soon divorced.

In 1970, Buchanan wrote to the executive editor of the *Herald* to inform him that as of August 14 of that year, she would have had five years of newspaper experience. Her letter ended with, "How about it?" He hired her.

Her first reporting included a ban on Miami Beach houseboats, North Bay village fire-fighting equipment that was dangerously antiquated, a Hialeah garbage strike, an appeal to Golda Meir on behalf of Israel bonds, the inadvertent poisonings of Miami Beach police dogs by insecticide, the clout of senior power and the arrival of the aardvark at the zoo.

Buchanan soon gained the reputation for being early at the scene of a disaster or unusual event. Once a reporter mentioned to his editor that he had just passed a burning Volkswagen on the expressway. Infuriated that the reporter had failed to investigate, the editor yelled at him that had Edna Buchanan seen the Volks, she would right now be talking on the phone to Germany, interviewing the assembly-line worker who put it together.

During her second year with the *Herald*, Buchanan learned much by covering criminal court. She became convinced that newspaper stories can get people out of jail or put them into jail; they can even change the law.

After reading that a wealthy Miami Beach socialite, convicted of two murders and sentenced to two life terms, had been quietly paroled to another state after only five years, she wrote a three-piece series on the parole system in Florida. At its next session, the legislature decreed that those convicted of first-degree murder must serve a mandatory minimum of 25 years before parole.

The court experience made Buchanan realize that good stories could be missed by general-assignment reporting, and she suggested to her editor that a reporter make daily visits to the major police departments, read the reports, rap with the troop, and then drop by the morgue and jail to check the overnight arrivals. The upshot was that in 1973, she was assigned to cover the police beat. At the time, few women were sent out on police stories.

Later in a 1996 interview, she recalled that at first cops, customs agents, F.B.I. and Coast Guard personnel were surprised at her presence at often gruesome events; in time, they did not even notice her, because she was always there She found that sometimes being a woman was an advantage in that a macho-type cop might prefer to give secrets to a woman rather than to a male reporter.

She worked very hard, always afraid that she would miss a story. Once on the scene, she wanted to know every detail, and this involved endless checking. She met deadlines. She always kept in mind that what mattered most was tomorrow's story. She enjoyed it because, according to her, it was a chance to try to learn about people with regard to sex, greed, violence, and passion, as well as what brings out the best in people and what makes them go berserk. She wrote about cops, good and bad; about cab drivers; about rape, drug dealing and about unsolved murders. The latter especially haunted her, for she likes to pursue problems to the finish.

"I want to know what the heck happened," she once told an interviewer. She certainly did not lack material to write about. Beginning in the 1970s, Miami saw a surge in the availability of illicit drugs and also an influx of illegal immigrants. In 1980–81, that city had the highest murder rate in the United States.

Her stories showed great sympathy for victims and their families. She has noted that the victim is history, old news, a name on a piece of paper. This is in contrast to the flesh-and-blood human being standing before judges, juries and parole commissions. Her concern may be related to her feelings about gun control: "I think the American people have a right to defend themselves. A lot of times the cavalry doesn't get there in time, as in so many cases I've covered as a reporter."

Buchanan holds that the reporter can be the victim's best friend—an article can get the victim donations of various types and also win public support, which can often lead to justice. In an interview, she said, "It is a brutal fact of life that a case reported in the newspaper, that gets the spotlight of publicity, is better investigated by the police, better prosecuted, and the judges are far less likely to make a deal. So often we can be responsible for justice triumphing in a case where it never would have otherwise."

On December 21, 1979, she first reported on the motorcycle death of Arthur Lee McDuffie, 33, a black insurance executive. Through an unnamed female source she knew that he was dead because of police brutality, and that there had been a cover up to make it appear an accident. Her reporting led to the indictment of five white police officers.

When the police officers were later released, race riots erupted, which led to the deaths of 18 persons. The property damage in Miami was estimated at $100 million. Buchanan felt no guilt at what happened. She considered herself a bad-news messenger, the reporter who found out and wrote the true story.

Sometimes she reported bizarre events. Alex Monroe had been murdered and his body identified by his daughter. His family attended the open-coffin funeral. Four months later, after a stay in North Carolina, he appeared at his daughter's door. The explanation was that there were two Alex Monroes; each was 62, each the size of the other, each had a scar on the left side of the face.

Mamie Higgs, the daughter who made the identification, had borrowed from a credit union to pay for her father's funeral. Buchanan, who often helped victims' relatives, tried to help Mrs. Higgs to recover the funeral money from the undertaker. The best she could do was a get a promise that when Higgs' father departed this life, that undertaker would provide free services.

A conference of women journalists, in which Gloria Steinem participated, stimulated Buchanan to inquire whether she and a male reporter were receiving comparable recompense. She was not pleased to learn that he was making $100 more per week than she.

At the very beginning of her reporting career, Buchanan wore heels and dressy clothes; she soon changed to more utilitarian attire. In fact, she kept a pair of fireman's boots handy. Also, she always had a police scanner in her car. It is obvious that her writing occupied a major part of her life.

*Carr: Five Years of Rape and Murder: From the Personal Account of Robert Frederick Carr III* was Buchanan's first book, published in 1979. Carr, convicted of rape and murder, wanted Buchanan to tell his story in the hope that it might help others. *Carr* did not sell well, which for some time discouraged the author from writing another book.

Buchanan's productivity did not go unnoticed. During the 1970s, she received awards from the American Bar Association, the National Newspapers Association and the Florida Society of Newspapers. In 1982, the Society of Professional Journalists gave her their Green Eye Shade Award for deadline reporting. Three years later, she won a big one: the Pulitzer Prize for general reporting.

Between 1973 and 1988, Buchanan wrote the stories behind more than 5,000 violent crimes, most of them murders. The *New Yorker* interviewed her in 1986, making this observation: "In Miami, a few figures are discussed by first name among people they have never actually met. One of them is Fidel. Another is Edna."

On receiving a contract to write a true account of her life as a crime reporter, she took a leave of absence. That work, *The Corpse Had a Familiar Face: Covering Miami, America's Hottest Beat*, published by Random House in 1987, was a best seller. The *New York Times* reviewer termed it honest and noted the "brave reporting." It was adapted for a television film.

In view of this success, Buchanan asked for another leave from the *Herald* to write a novel—something she had wanted to do since childhood. *Nobody Lives Forever* came out in 1990, receiving mixed reviews. The leave from her newspaper job became permanent. Her next endeavor was *Never Let Them See You Cry; More from Miami, America's Hottest Beat*. It was a sort of addition to *The Corpse*.

Buchanan's second novel, published in 1992, introduced a series featuring Britt Montero. After years of intense focus on exact detail, evident in her crime reporting, she began to write fiction with some doubts and fears.

Eventually she enjoyed not being tied to using the exact date, the sequence of events and so on. And she does not have to leave crimes unsolved—all the pieces can come together, thanks to her imagination. "It's absolutely wonderful," she said. Regarding fiction, Ross Lockridge's *Raintree County* is her favorite book of all time.

When Buchanan had lived in Miami for more than a quarter of a century, she told an interviewer that she is still excited her to see banana trees growing in her backyard and palm trees outlined against the sky and the water.

She continues to live in her beloved Miami with her beloved cats. And she continues to turn out successful fiction.

Britt Montero, a blond with blue eyes, is a Cuban-American staff reporter for the *Miami Daily News*. When she was 3, her Cuban father was executed by a Castro firing squad. Her mother's English forbearers were Miami pioneers. When hired, she was considered bilingual. However, this assumption was questioned when vice mayor became mayor of vice.

Britt has a fierce love of Miami; she was miserable in Chicago during the two years she spent in that northern clime, studying journalism at Northwestern University. She can always find interesting cases to report—for example, a black football star dead at the hands of the police, supposedly for resisting arrest. Race riots follow. She deals with a murder that took place 22 years before, the number one suspect being a current candidate for mayor. She is present when a bomb and a hurricane devastate Miami.

At one point in her career, she herself becomes a murder suspect. She even kills a man in self-defence. She has an on-and-off relationship with a police officer named Kendall McDonald. Her mother wishes her daughter would pay more attention to her social life, but Britt seems wed to her career. She makes many statements that sound very much like the utterances of Edna Buchanan in the two books that are considered her memoirs. Here are two quotations from *Margin of Error*:

> But death seals lips. Nobody speaks for [the dead], so it was my job to find out all I could, then tell their stories in black and white, printed in our consciousness.
>
> But every once in a while, there comes a story. A story that blows your mind. One where you know you've made a difference. That's what makes it all worthwhile. That and the anticipation.

With regard to the critics who say that Britt is obviously her alter ego, Buchanan told an interviewer that Montero is what she, Buchanan, would like to be—agile and athletic and brave and beautiful, a woman of action, and not the klutz and note taker that the real writer claims she is.

I disagree. Edna Buchanan is surely a woman of action in her own way.

## *Listing of Works by Edna Buchanan*

Edna Buchanan does not use a pseudonym

### Britt Montero Series

*Contents Under Pressure* . . . . . . . . . . 1992
*Miami, It's Murder* . . . . . . . . . . 1994
*Suitable for Framing* . . . . . . . . . . 1995
*Act of Betrayal* . . . . . . . . . . 1996
*Margin of Error* . . . . . . . . . . 1997
*Garden of Evil* . . . . . . . . . . 1999

### Other Crime Fiction

*Nobody Lives Forever* . . . . . . . . . . 1990
*Pulse* . . . . . . . . . . 1998

### Nonfiction

*Carr: Five Years of Rape and Murder: From the Personal Account of Robert Frederick Car III* . . . . . . . . . . 1979
*The Corpse Had a Familiar Face: Covering Miami, America's Hottest Beat* . . . . . . . . . . 1987
*Never Let them See You Cry: More from Miami, America's Hotttest Beat* . . . . . . . . . . 1992

(Contributor to magazines)

# 15
# Kate Gallison

This author presents two series, varied in background, but witty, entertaining, and original.

Kathleen (Kate) Gallison was born on November 14, 1939, in Philadelphia to Herbert E. and Georgena (Hill) Gallison. Her salesman father did freelance writing. Dorothy was raised in Illinois and New Jersey, Herbert's work necessitating frequent moves for his family. According to *Contemporary Authors*, young Kate began to create stories in kindergarten just as soon as she could read and write letters. Before she had mastered cursive writing, she printed what she terms a science fiction novel entitled *Master Mechanic*. It dealt with a mad scientist who made human beings from salt. (The book is lost.) Over the years, she wrote other stories, shorter in length.

When in the fifth grade, she was influenced by an author who wrote very funny stories for *America Legion Magazine*. She cannot remember his name, but she knows that she copied his style. As a high school student, she imitated P.G. Wodehouse. In the 10th grade, she wrote an English comedy, but could not get it produced. She read mysteries, including Manning Coles. She recalls that for a time she thought of herself as a secret English person and used English spellings.

Kate studied at Douglass College, Rutgers University, from 1957–60. When the literary magazine rejected her serious works, she started a cartoon strip in the college paper. She had originally wanted o be a cartoonist, but dropped the idea because she could not draw well.

In 1966, she married Samuel Graff, by whom she had two sons. The marriage ended in divorce in 1975. Seven years later, a reference librarian named Harold E. Dunn became Kate's second husband. That marriage produced one son.

Kate has had a variety of careers: a short stint as a library clerk for the *Washington Post* and as an accounting clerk for American Telephone and Telegraph Company. For the years 1961–1974, she lists herself as housewife, amateur actress, cartoonist, puppeteer and sales clerk. Then she was employed for five years as clerk-bookkeeper for the New Jersey Division of Youth and Family Services. The next five years saw her working as computer program-analyst at New Jersey's Department of the Treasury in Trenton. Later she was a technical writer at Applied Data Research in Princeton.

She completed requisites for a B.A. degree at Thomas A. Edison College (now State College) in Trenton in 1979. After leaving Douglass College, Gallison wrote occasional short pieces for newspapers. She concedes that Erma Bombeck did it better. Gradually her style improved, and she found herself rid of Wodehouse's influence.

*Unbalanced Accounts*, her first book, came out in 1986. It introduced Nick Magaracz and became the first in a series of three. According to the author, she set *Unbalanced Accounts* in Trenton because she had lived there for 18 years and knew the community. She looked at the state government and then took sidelong glances at New Jersey life in general.

A second series featuring an Episcopalian priest named Mother Lavinia Grey was begun in 1995 with *Bury the Bishop*.

Gallison lives in Lambertville, New Jersey, with her husband.

The reader first meets Nick when he is a private detective in Trenton. A graduate of Trenton Catholic Boys' High and a Korean War veteran, he yearns to investigate industrial espionage. But he has not been inundated with exotic cases—or even mundane ones; in fact, cases are scarce.

His wife Ethel has a cousin, Charlie Del Pietro, who works for the New Jersey Bureau of Mental Rehabilitation as officer manager of Accounts Receivable. When 375 checks are missing, Charlie offers Nick the job of investigating their disappearance. Since no money has been appropriated for the services of a detective, Nick is hired as an accountant, a position that is open. Nick knows nothing about accounting, but he does "a revolting thing": he heeds Ethel's advice to take a job with the state, where he would have a good life and a steady paycheck.

He does not solve the mystery of the missing checks, but helps with crimes associated with it. The job involves putting up with the noise of adding machines and listening to details about the hysterectomies of some of the office workers rather than dealing with the machinations of spies.

But even these inconveniences do not deter him from taking another job with the state. According to his thinking, it was not easy to leave "the warm bosom of Mother Civil Service," and the state dental service would pay for daughter Amy's braces.

Thus, *The Death Tape* sees Nick employed by the Bureau of Tax Enforcement, where he is to ascertain who cheated on paying inheritance taxes. His adventures there include contact with a radical right-wing tax revolt organization. The latter is a local ethnic group invented by Gallison.

The last in the series, *The Jersey Monkey*, has Nick in contact with the rich and powerful of Trenton, as he witnesses corporate graft and drug testing on animals.

The writing is humorous satire/parody of bureaucratic procedures and of detective fiction.

The sleuth of the second series is Mother Vinnie, a counselor and the vicar of St. Bede's Episcopal Church in Fisherville, New Jersey. (Gallison is herself an Episcopalian.) Vinnie's life has not been easy; her parents were killed in an accident and she was raised by a grandmother; her husband dies. St. Bede's is not the plum of parishes—there is always some problem at hand to absorb Vinnie's energy. For example, the bishop of the diocese, to whom she is responsible, had been trying to close St. Bede's. And with some justification: the congregation numbers fewer than ten and there has not been a baptism in thirty years. When he is murdered at a church convention, the priest herself and her delegates are under suspicion. Vinnie solves that matter, only to find other problems such as a headless corpse and a case that reveals bigamy. It is not surprising that she has no time to watch TV and does not want a set in the rectory.

Slight and delicate in appearnace, she is loved by many. She has a social conscience and takes to heart most of Fisherville's problems, which are numerous. "We look out for each other here," she says. She supports gun control, making her church a collecting point for citizens to turn in their arms. One of her pet causes is the plight of the homeless.

The books mention contemporary events of the 1990s, such as cellular phones, a kid with blue hair and jewels in his nose, and a computer consultant who specializes in the year 2000.

Here are some of Gallison's remarks that apply to the religious life. About a seminary graduate: "Late vocation. Her children were grown, her husband had run off with some tootsie from his office, so she had turned to the Lord." About the life to come: "...when the pie was dished up in the sky."

About a church convention: "And there was no requirement that the delegates have all their buttons."

In 1998, Mother Vinnie is 39 and an accomplished cellist; she has an old flame working at the police department in Trenton (introduced in *Bury the Bishop)* and she is still full of energy and ideas. It is just possible that Gallison will produce more of those witty accounts of the vicar's exploits—depictions that so delight her Mother Vinnie fans.

## *Listing of Works by Kate Gallison*

Kate Gallison does not use a pseudonym

### Mother Lavinia Gray Series

*Bury the Bishop* .......... 1995
*The Devil's Workshop* .......... 1996
*Unholy Angels* .......... 1996
*Hasty Retreat* .......... 1997
*Grave Misgivings* .......... 1998

### Nick Magaracz Series

*Unbalanced Accounts* .......... 1986
*The Death Tape* .......... 1987
*The Jersey Monkey* .......... 1992

# 16
# Sue Grafton

Detective story fans hail her as an innovator of the Tough Girl Private Eye.

Sue Grafton was born April 24, 1940, in Louisville, Kentucky, to Chip Warren Grafton and Vivian Boisseau (Harnsberger) Grafton. Her father was an attorney and a writer; her mother taught high school chemistry. In 1961, Sue graduated from the University of Louisville with a major in English.

She began to write when she was 22. Her writer father, author of three mysteries and a standard novel, had some influence on her career. He explained to her how to deal with rejection, and he imparted to her how to write with clarity and simplicity. He did not believe in revising the English language. Sue remembered that G.W. Grafton considered it a miracle that a writer's thoughts could be translated into symbols on a page and then enter someone else's head. He impressed her that a writer must pay attention to transitions and minor characters, as well as to the big scenes and main characters. Sue has read her father's *Beyond a Reasonable Doubt* (1950) numerous times. He died in 1982 before his literary aspirations were reached.

His daughter's first published book came out in 1967. It was a novel about the Depression, but when Sue began it, she knew nothing about that era. She soon learned the importance of background research. Two years later, a second novel was published. Then, according to Grafton, "I did a long detour into movies-for-television." She had married for the first time, moved to California and would be involved for 10 years in writing screenplays and teleplays. The second novel was *The Lolly-Madonna War.* Set in Appalachia, it was made into a Metro-Goldwyn-Mayer film in

1973, with Sue writing the screenplay. By the spring of 1975, she was experienced enough to write an episode for the popular TV situation comedy *Rhoda.* Later on, she wrote several TV scripts with the man who became her third husband. She grew accustomed to being paid very well for this type of work. Also, television writing taught her to be economical and concrete. However, she disliked the "writing by committee" work that she had been doing and felt the need to get back to solo writing.

The mystery proved the looked-for antidote to the Hollywood work, which she continued at the same time. Her first detective story was *"A" Is for Alibi,* published in 1982. Grafton told an interviewer that this book is partly based on a scheme she had devised to kill an ex-husband, with whom she was involved in a custody battle. (Good sense prevailed over her carrying out such a plan.) *Alibi* launched the alphabet series with Kinsey Millhone as the principal investigator. Three years later, *"B" Is for Burglar* appeared, and following that, one series book a year. These mysteries have been very popular, with Grafton active in their promotion. Winning numerous awards, they have been translated into several languages, including Dutch, Russian, Polish, Spanish and French. *"Z" Is for Zero* should appear by 2009.

Grafton says the great struggle of her life is learning how to plot—character and dialogue are easier for her. She enjoys doing the research required and hopes she does not show off when she returns the knowledge to her reader. She likes to write a paragraph of prose that is succinct and evocative. Her submissions to the editor require little editing. With regard to other writers, she admires the works of Elmore Leonard, Dick Francis, Ruth Rendell, and Agatha Christie—the latter for her cleverness, but not for character development. She likes Ross Macdonald but notes that he tends to tell one story again and again. She has learned from Tony Hillerman. She views the mystery as a vantage point from which to observe the world we live in. She believes that the author's job is to entertain in the best sense of the word.

When asked how much of Sue Grafton is in Kinsey Millhone, the author admits that the private eye is a stripped-down version of herself—thinner, younger and braver—the person Grafton would have been had she not married young and had three children.

She is a member of Mystery Writers of America, serving as president in 1994–95, and of the Crime Writers Association of Great Britain. She dislikes gender-segregated awards, contending in a 1992 interview:

> To me, writing is not about gender, and to me to imply that women are in any way at a disadvantage seems incorrect.... I don't see women as victims. I don't see women as one down. I don't believe we need to herd

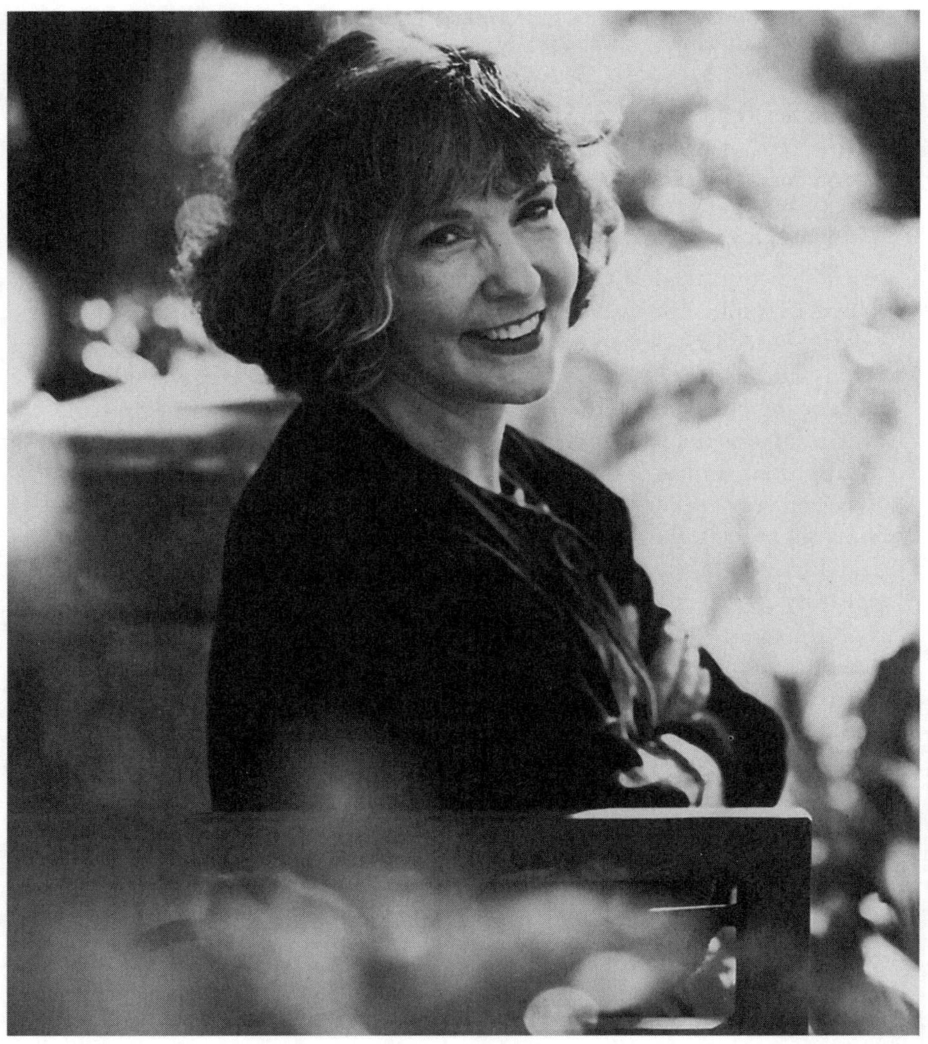

**Sue Grafton by Bill Reitzel. By courtesy of Henry Holt.**

> together in order to have power in the world. So what I prefer to do is to operate out of my own system, wherein, in some ways, I think I'm doing just as much for women by being out on the front lines by myself.

Steven F. Humphrey, a professor of philosophy, became Grafton's third husband in 1978. She is now a grandmother. Her avocational interests are listed as walking, reading, cooking and bridge.

Page 2 of *"C" Is for Corpse* quotes Kinsey Millhone describing Santa Teresa Fitness as smelling like men's jockstraps. From the beginning of an alphabet book, the reader realizes that this type of language is characteristic of Millhone—a sleuth far removed from Miss Marple in speech, mannerisms, outlook, and life style.

Kinsey—that was her grandmother's maiden name—lost her parents in an automobile accident when she was five years old. Raised primarily in trailer parks by her unmarried Aunt Gin, she has a dislike of formal schooling. By the time she was 25, she was the proprietor of Kinsey Millhone Investigations in the fictional town of Santa Teresa, California, 95 miles north of Los Angeles (said to resemble Santa Barbara). Before being on her own, she had served for one year on the police force in Santa Teresa, where about 85 percent of all criminal homicides are resolved. She had left because in those days, "...policewomen were viewed with a mixture of curiosity and scorn." She had also held several noninvestigative jobs. A private investigator's license required 4000 hours spent in apprenticeship. This she did with a small detective firm. Millhone Investigations rents office space in a law firm and has had many years of success. Kinsey's strong point is interview; she is cautious and not inclined to jump into a situation without adequate background. She informs the reader that an unpracticed liar can't always rise to the occasion as she can. Her charge is $50 an hour plus expenses.

Millhone ages slowly—for example, in a book copyrighted in 1985, she is 32, and in one copyrighted 10 years later, she is only 35. Millhone is 5 feet, 6 inches and has hazel eyes. By the time she reaches 35, she is twice divorced; her first husband is a drug abuser,* her second a mother's boy. Millhone is also a woman without children, plants or house pets. She jogs six days a week. She wears jeans, a turtleneck sweater and Reeboks. She has an "all purpose black dress" made of polyester and it cannot be crushed. She disdains high heels. She owns a Volkswagen and has $25,000 in a savings account.

"I love being single," Milhone states, "It's almost like being rich." She does form a friendly relationship with her octogenarian landlord, from whom she rents a studio apartment. (She had been in a trailer court until those under 55 were no longer welcome.) A retired baker, Henry, the landlord, caters tea parties for old ladies and writes crossword puzzles. Millhone says if he were younger, she would grab him for herself. She is not at first inclined to become friendly with some newfound relatives.

**In* "O" Is for Outlaw *(1999) new evidence surfaces that puts former vice cop Micky Magruder in a more favorable light than Kinsey saw him at the time of the divorce.*

*"L" Is for Lawless* exemplifies Grafton's aim to keep Millhone "flawed and inconsistent." As are many of the alphabet mysteries, it is written from the Millhone viewpoint.

As a favor to Henry, Kinsey sets out to find out why Johnny Lee, a neighbor who has died, is not eligible for military burial despite the fact that Johnny had been a pilot under Claire Chennault during World War II. Kinsey remarks as an aside that the Lees are not classy folks unless a car up on blocks is your notion of a yard ornament. When Lee's empty apartment is broken into and later on, one of his friends severely beaten, Kinsey knows that something serious is happening.

When she is on her way to a supermarket to pick up milk and oven cleaner for a neighbor, she sees a man wearing a black Stetson hat leave the supposedly empty apartment with a large duffel bag. On a hunch, she follows him and sees him pick up a woman. The two drive to the airport, followed by Millhone. The woman, duffel bag in hand, boards a plane for Palm Beach.

Kinsey barely has time to call John Lee's son Chester, who authorizes her return plane fare from Santa Teresa to Palm Beach. With her she has only the clothes she is wearing plus her California driver's license, her P.I. license, two major credit cards (one of which has expired and the other with a large current balance), $46.52 in cash, a telephone charge card, an ATM card (good only in California). She also has key picks, toothbrush and toothpaste, clean underpants, Swiss Army knife, sunglasses, comb, lipstick, corkscrew, two pens, and aspirin and birth control pills, plus a mystery key found in Lee's hidden safe. Unfortunately, her check book is on her desk at home.

Thanksgiving is just days away, and Kinsey is scheduled to be a bridesmaid at a Thanksgiving Day wedding in Santa Teresa. The bride is close to 70, the groom 88. Kinsey, at 35, is one of two bridesmaids; the other is 95. Even if most of the principals are suitable subjects for geriatric study, Millhone will be back for the event, for, come what may; she is noted for her reliability. (She will be forgiven if the neighbor had to go one night without milk for supper and the oven didn't get cleaned for another day.)

Millhone is lucky enough to get a seat across the aisle and two rows forward from the woman with the duffel bag—a woman who looks pregnant. When the woman leaves her seat, the sleuth makes a rapid search. She also follows the duffel-bag passenger when she debarks at the Dallas–Fort Worth airport, before the completion of the flight. The woman goes to a hotel, with Millhone in pursuit.

It is not always smooth sailing; for instance, after helping herself to a chambermaid's uniform from the laundry, she gains entrance to the woman's room. However, when a security guard notices that Kinsey's Reeboks are not regulation, Millhone realizes that she is going to need more ingenuity—in other words, she must think up more of the usual lies and deceits. To complicate matters, now other people, once involved with Lee, are appearing on the scene.

Millhone deduces that Lee was never in the armed services; rather he was in prison, and that some of the recent arrivals to Texas had also been convicts. They are there to have a cut in the cache of valuables that they knew Lee had acquired from a bank and secreted. It is Millhone who helps to solve the problem of the keys that ultimately open a Lawless family mausoleum in Louisville, Kentucky, the spot where the major part of the heist is hidden. It is also Millhone who guesses that Laura, the woman with the duffel bag, is not pregnant; that her increased girth is due to around $8000 in bills that her abusive common-law husband had stolen from Lee's apartment and carried out in the duffel bag.

It cannot be said that Kinsey, for all her ingenuity, sees justice done. At best, the meanest of the criminals—the man in the Stetson—is killed. The most likable turns out to be Laura's father. But he disappears with her, his feisty mother and the loot to parts unknown.

One bonus of Kinsey's adventure is a reconciliation with some members of her family. Her well-to-do mother had run away with a mailman, and apparently her maternal relatives had had little to do with her or her Aunt Gin, now dead. Through professional contacts, she had learned about the existence of her cousin Tasha Howard, an estate attorney. When Tasha had invited Kinsey to spend Thanksgiving with the the whole family, she had been glad to have the excuse of the wedding for her not going. However, when stranded in Louisville the day before Thanksgiving and unable to rouse anyone she knew, the PI remembered that Tasha had told her to call if she ever needed anything.

Kinsey did just that. And she arrived at the wedding on time.

## *Listing of Works by Sue Grafton*

PSEUDONYM: No pseudonym used

---

### KINSEY MILLHONE SERIES

"A" *Is for Alibi* . . . . . . . . . . . . . . . . . . . . . . . . . . . . . . . . . . . . . . . . . .1982
"B" *Is for Burglar* . . . . . . . . . . . . . . . . . . . . . . . . . . . . . . . . . . . . . . .1985
"C" *Is for Corpse* . . . . . . . . . . . . . . . . . . . . . . . . . . . . . . . . . . . . . . . .1986

*"D" Is for Deadbeat* . . . . . . . . . . . . . . . . . . . . . . . . . . . . . . . . . . . . . . . . .1987
*"E" Is for Evidence* . . . . . . . . . . . . . . . . . . . . . . . . . . . . . . . . . . . . . . . . . .1988
*"F" Is for Fugitive* . . . . . . . . . . . . . . . . . . . . . . . . . . . . . . . . . . . . . . . . . .1989
*"G" Is for Gumshoe* . . . . . . . . . . . . . . . . . . . . . . . . . . . . . . . . . . . . . . . . .1990
*"H" Is for Homicide* . . . . . . . . . . . . . . . . . . . . . . . . . . . . . . . . . . . . . . . . .1991
*"I" Is for Innocent* . . . . . . . . . . . . . . . . . . . . . . . . . . . . . . . . . . . . . . . . . .1992
*"J" Is for Judgment* . . . . . . . . . . . . . . . . . . . . . . . . . . . . . . . . . . . . . . . . . .1993
*"K" Is for Killer* . . . . . . . . . . . . . . . . . . . . . . . . . . . . . . . . . . . . . . . . . . . .1994
*"L" Is for Lawless* . . . . . . . . . . . . . . . . . . . . . . . . . . . . . . . . . . . . . . . . . . .1995
*"M" Is for Malice* . . . . . . . . . . . . . . . . . . . . . . . . . . . . . . . . . . . . . . . . . . .1997
*"N" Is for Noose* . . . . . . . . . . . . . . . . . . . . . . . . . . . . . . . . . . . . . . . . . . . .1998
*"O" Is for Outlaw* . . . . . . . . . . . . . . . . . . . . . . . . . . . . . . . . . . . . . . . . . . .1999

### SHORT STORIES

*Kinsey and Me* . . . . . . . . . . . . . . . . . . . . . . . . . . . . . . . . . . . . . . . . . . . . .1992

### OTHER FICTION

*Keziah Dane* . . . . . . . . . . . . . . . . . . . . . . . . . . . . . . . . . . . . . . . . . . . . . . .1967
*The Lolly-Madonna War* . . . . . . . . . . . . . . . . . . . . . . . . . . . . . . . . . . . . . . .1969

### NONFICTION

Editor, *Writing Mysteries: A Handbook* . . . . . . . . . . . . . . . . . . . . . . . . . . . .1992

(Contributor of scripts to television series)

# 17

# Sara Paretsky

When Sara Paretsky's agent tried to sell *Indemnity Only*, he found that publishers were dubious about whether her independent private eye named V.I. Warshawski would find an audience. Paretsky's book sold, and within a year of its publication, Sue Grafton's first book was out. After that, the popularity of the modern female investigator was established with detective story fans.

Sara Paretsky was born on June 8, 1947, in Ames, Iowa. Her parents were David Paretsky, a scientist, and Mary (Edwards) Paretsky, a librarian. Even when a young child, Sara liked to write; she recalls persuading her brothers, then of early elementary-school age, to act in a play that she had written. But it was much later in her life that she aspired to be a writer.

Sara grew up in Kansas, where, according to her, "girls didn't grow up to work, they grew up to be mommies." In 1967, she graduated summa cum laude from the University of Kansas with a major in political science. During the summer of her sophomore year, she had worked in Chicago, the city with which her name is associated. She told an interviewer, "That was at the height of all the social-actions movements. Like many people, I felt an ardent desire to be involved in the great problems of our day, and I came here to work in a project in the inner city." She was 19, on her own for the first time, and becoming so involved in the city made a permanent impression on her.

After graduation from college, Paretsky settled in Chicago. By 1977, she had two degrees from the University of Chicago: a MBA and a Ph.D. in history. She was employed for ten years as a marketing manager by the insurance company Continental National America.

On June 19, 1976, Paretsky married Professor Courtney Wright. They are the parents of Kimball, Timothy and Philip. Paretsky and her husband, now grandparents, still live in Chicago, with their golden retriever.

So Sara Paretsky grew up to work *and* to be a mommy.

Here (from a personal communication) is her explanation of why she started writing mystery novels:

"For many years I read crime fiction in preference to any other kind of fiction. This engagement with that genre dates back to my early teen-years. In fact, when I was at the University of Chicago working on my doctoral dissertation in history, I read twenty-nine crime novels the month before I was to take my doctor's orals. As a result of this interest, it was natural for me to turn to crime fiction when I wanted to try to write my own novel.

"In addition, as I became a more aware feminist and began analyzing the roles that women played in crime fiction, I began to feel a strong wish to change those dominating images. In general, in American crime fiction of the 30s through the 70s, women were either sexually active and therefore instantly identifiable as evil, or sexually chaste, in which case they could not act at all. In fact, I see that these roles dominate Western views of women throughout fiction but of course I was mainly aware of them in crime fiction. It took me about eight years of many false starts before I came up with the character of V.I. Warshawski. Her first adventure was published in 1982 as *Indemnity Only.*"

The setting would be Chicago and would involve the insurance business. By so doing, she could avoid necessary and time-consuming research because both Chicago and the insurance business were well known to her.

Chicago has a large Polish-American population and Paretsky herself is part Polish so she sought a Polish name for her character. She created Warshawski from Warsaw. The initials V.I. seemed to go with it, so she picked the names Victoria and Iphegenia for them to represent.

According to Paretsky, her protagonist–P.I. looks beyond the surface to "...where power and money corrupt people into making criminal decisions to preserve their position. All of her cases explore some aspect of white collar crime where some executives preserve position or bolster their companies without regard for the ordinary people who work for them."

The first of what became the Warshawski series was dedicated to Stuart Kaminsky. Paretsky had taken an extension course from him at Northwestern University, and he had given her the confidence she needed to finish the book. Another book was dedicated to Pattie Shephard, Paretsky's fourth grade teacher, and to Jayanne Angell and Bill Mullins, two of her high school teachers. Paretsky also gives the women's movement credit for her accomplishment.

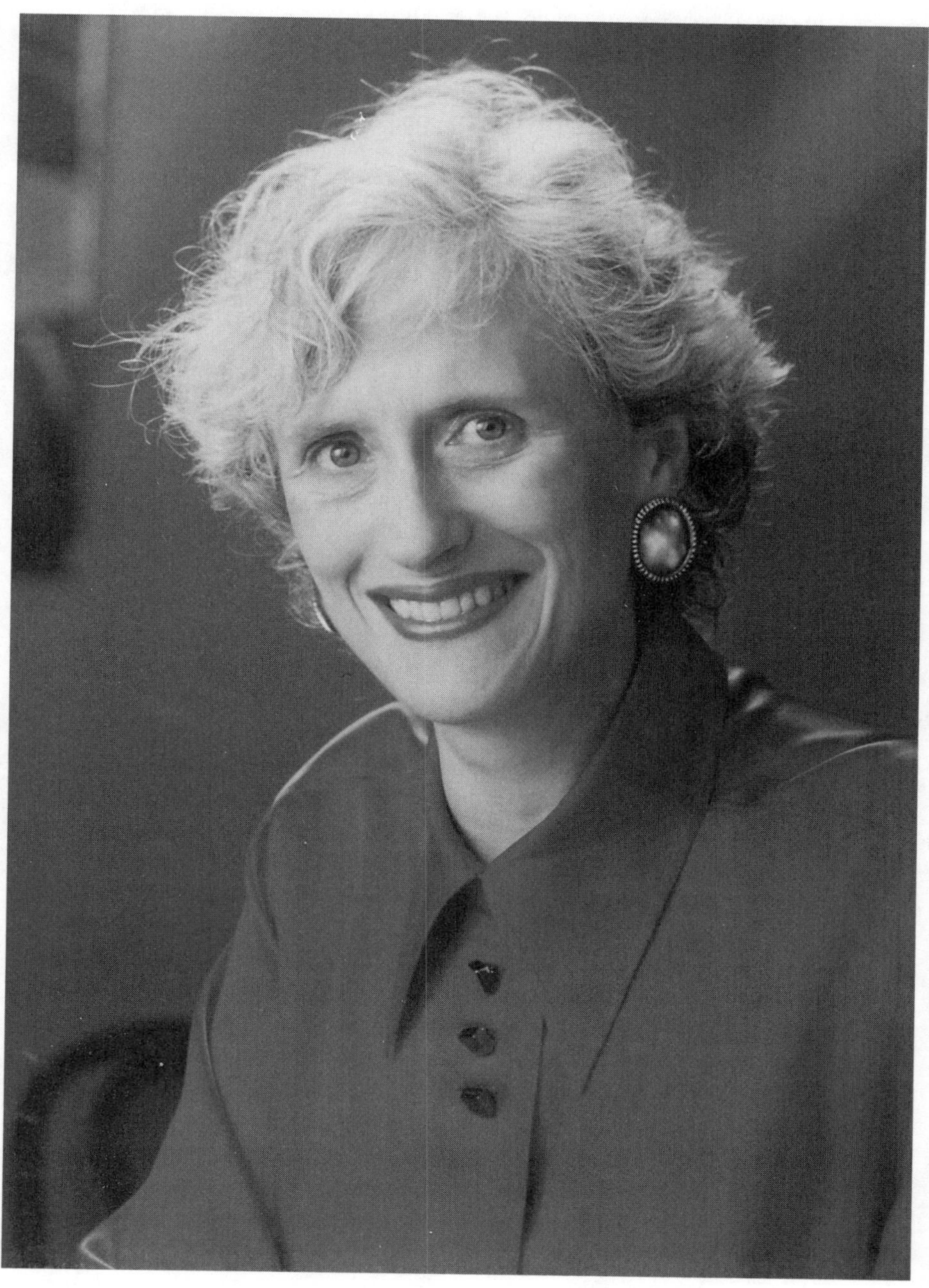

Sara Paretsky by Will Crockett. By courtesy of Sara Paretsky.

Despite the fact that Paretsky's brother is a priest in the Dominican Order, her thinking is not always in accord with the views of the Roman Catholic Church, and she does not flinch from stating them.

The series books have been very popular, with *Blood Shot* winning a Silver Dagger. By 1999, almost six million of Paretsky's *New York Times* bestseller novels were in print, with foreign editions printed in 21 countries. *Indemnity Only* was adapted into the film *V.I. Warshawsky*. According to K.G. Klein, the movie is far below the caliber of the book. Paretsky also writes short stories and essays and has edited collections of mystery stories by women. Her 1998 book entitled *Ghost Country* was not part of the series.

Paretsky wrote three books while she was still working as a marketing manager. The success of her writing meant that she was able to leave her demanding job to devote herself full time to writing.

After the publication of *Ghost Country,* Paretsky's web site conducted a contest, "Where is V.I. Warshawski?" Participants were invited to submit entries under various guidelines, with the prizes signed pre-publication copies of *Hard Time*, in which V.I. comes back.

Paretsky is proud of her role in Sisters in Crime. The organization's role is to promote more reviews of mysteries written by women and to scrutinize the portrayals of women characters in the genre. Considerable progress has been made in both these areas. Sisters in Crime now has more than 3,000 members worldwide.

Paretsky founded two scholarships at her alma mater in Kansas, and she mentors students in Chicago's inner city schools. She reports that she enjoys singing, running and good whiskey. She has received numerous awards, including the 1996 Mark Twain Award for "distinguished contributions to Midwestern literature," and a Visiting Scholarship to Oxford University in 1997.

This popular mystery writer appreciates the support she receives from her readers; she has heard from women from Tokyo to Chicago's South Side that reading about V.I. has given them courage to face difficulties in their own lives. That, she once said, is a strong impetus to keep writing about her P.I.

V.I. tells her story in the first person. Mention of specific events, people and so on date the writing—for instance, there is a reference to the television show *General Hospital,* to Oliver North, to Mayor Washington of Chicago, to Kosovo, to espresso, to roller blades. Also, words such as upscale appear.

Victoria Warshawski, who has olive skin, dark curly hair and good legs, specializes in financial crime in Chicago. A feminist and an activist, she is also an attorney. Her spunky Italian mother and her police-officer father are dead. She remembers that they loved her and encouraged her to believe she could succeed at anything she wanted to. (At 10, they saw she had a savings account. She went to the University of Chicago on an athletic scholarship.) A mother-substitute of sorts is Dr. Charlotte Herschel, her physician. A neighbor named Contreras gives fatherly advice and helps care for her two retrievers. A Cubs fan, V.I. is a runner and adamantly opposed to smoking, the habit that contributed to her father's demise. She is not, however, opposed to alcohol. She is divorced, and seems more interested in her profession than in marriage.

Among other cases, she is involved in searching for a woman missing from the University of Chicago; in investigating the death of a hockey player while he was working at the city docks; in solving the disappearance of stock certificates from a monastery. She is instrumental in exposing malpractice in medicine, corruption in politics and so on. Issues such as homelessness and abortion come up.

It is clear that Warshawski sides with the underdog, as is well illustrated in *Blood Shot*. She was aware that a young unmarried girl had been thrown out when her parents found that she was pregnant. When V.I. discovers that the baby's father is the girl's maternal uncle, and that the parents blamed their daughter for not discouraging her uncle's "weakness," her reaction is unusually intense—anger at the parents and sympathy for the daughter.

When V.I. comes back in *Hard Time*, she is approaching 45. (Her age does not prevent her from jumping from a building onto a moving freight train.) Finances are a continuing problem; she is prone to involve herself in cases that merit solving, but that hold little promise of bringing in needed revenue. In this book, she investigates the death of Nicola Aguinaldo, an illegal immigrant from the Philippines, who was imprisoned for theft. Warshawski's activities landed her in a fictional experimental women's jail-cum-prison in Cools, Illinois—the same institution that had housed Nicola. Realizing that she might uncover valuable information about Nicola, V.I. refused bail. In resolving the case, she involves herself in the issues of corruption in politics, illegal profit from prison labor, sexual harassment of women prisoners, computer fraud and the power of the press.

V.I. Warshawski admits that sometimes she is foolhardy, daring without judgment. And sometimes her actions get her into serious trouble. But most importantly, she has integrity and compassion and does not break down under duress. All in all, she seems to be what her creator intended her to be.

## *Listing of Works by Sara Paretsky*

Sara Paretsky does not use a pseudonym

### V.I. Warshawski Series

*Indemnity Only* . . . . . . . . . . . . . . . . . . . . . . . . . . . . . . . . . .1982
*Deadlock* . . . . . . . . . . . . . . . . . . . . . . . . . . . . . . . . . . . . . .1984
*Killing Orders* . . . . . . . . . . . . . . . . . . . . . . . . . . . . . . . . . .1985
*Bitter Medicine* . . . . . . . . . . . . . . . . . . . . . . . . . . . . . . . . .1987
*Blood Shot* . . . . . . . . . . . . . . . . . . . . . . . . . . . . . . . . . . . .1988
(published in England as *Toxic Shock)*
*Burn Marks* . . . . . . . . . . . . . . . . . . . . . . . . . . . . . . . . . . . .1990
*Guardian Angel* . . . . . . . . . . . . . . . . . . . . . . . . . . . . . . . . .1991
*Tunnel Vision* . . . . . . . . . . . . . . . . . . . . . . . . . . . . . . . . . .1994
*Hard Time* . . . . . . . . . . . . . . . . . . . . . . . . . . . . . . . . . . . . .1999

### Crime Novel

*Ghost Country* . . . . . . . . . . . . . . . . . . . . . . . . . . . . . . . . . .1998

### Short Story Collections

*Windy City Blues* . . . . . . . . . . . . . . . . . . . . . . . . . . . . . . . .1995
Editor: *A Woman's Eye* . . . . . . . . . . . . . . . . . . . . . . . . . . . .1991
Editor: *Women on the Case* . . . . . . . . . . . . . . . . . . . . . . . . .1996

(Author of essays, contributor to periodicals)

# 18
# Nevada Barr

One accomplished mystery writer—Sara Paretsky—praised *A Superior Death* with these words: "Nevada Barr has brought my beloved Great Lakes to life. This is brilliant nature writing, with a beautifully crafted mystery as a bonus." This is the essence of Barr's writing—fine nature descriptions combined with absorbing mysteries.

Barr's first name is that of her native state, where she was born around 1952. She grew up in Susanville, California, where both her parents were airplane pilots at a small mountain airport; her sister Molly followed the family tradition by working as a commercial pilot. There were other strong women in the family: an Aunt Peggy taught third grade in a New York City public school, while Barr's grandmother has been described as a globe-trotting missionary as well as a fighting Quaker Democrat.

Barr has said of them, "These women did not come in at the second act to fluff up the pillows and leave."

Nevada received a B.A. degree from what is now California Polytechnical State University in San Luis Obispo, California, and an M.A. (in theater) from the University of California, Irvine.

For 18 years she pursued a career as an actress, performing in Off Broadway shows in New York, as well as in television commercials and corporate and industrial films in Minneapolis. During this time she married a fellow actor.

In 1989, this versatile woman joined the National Park Service as a law enforcement ranger. She and her husband both embraced the ideals of the environmental movement, and he had became an employee of the same agency. Before she worked full time as a writer, she saw service intermittently in various national park areas—Guadalupe Mountains in Texas,

Mesa Verde in Colorado, Natchez Trace Parkway in Mississippi, Horsefly Fire Camp in Idaho.

The beginning of her third career—that of an author—was marked by the writing of historical fiction. In 1984, her novel entitled *Bittersweet* was published. Not a crime novel, it dealt with a lesbian relationship; the characters settled in Nevada. The book was not a financial success.

Nine years later, her Anna Pigeon series began with the publication of *Tract of the Cat.* This won both Anthony and Agatha awards. Other crime novels appeared in the series, and more are expected.

Barr now lives with her second husband in Clinton, Mississippi.

Anna Pigeon is by training a park ranger, she is also an amateur sleuth because, according to her creator, she is the sort of person who has to take apart perfectly good clocks to see the inside. She attended college in San Luis Obispo. She has known sorrow—watching her father die of Lou Gehrig's disease and losing her actor husband Zach in an accident. The latter tragedy drove her to alcohol, and the reader is left with the impression that although the problem is under control, it is a potential danger. Her personal life is centered around her sister Molly, seven years older and a psychiatrist.

Pigeon becomes a National Park Service ranger, serving first in the Guadalupe Mountains National Park in west Texas where her companion was a saddle horse named Gideon. The mystery to be solved involves the death of a park ranger, thought to have been killed by a mountain lion.

Anna leaves Texas for Michigan's Isle Royale in Lake Superior. A scuba diver, her investigation takes her into that lake's frigid water. (Barr herself never dived in Lake Superior, but consulted Dan Lenihan, chief of the park services' Submerged Cultural Resources Unit.) Pigeon is now 40, not too old for an FBI agent named Frederick Stanton to come into her life. (Molly had pointed out that her sister's memory of Zach tolled the death knell for any relationship Anna might attempt with a man not perfect enough to be dead.)

At Mesa Verde National Park, where there are Anasazi cliff dwellings, Stanton and Anna work on solving the murder of a park ranger. Her next assignment is to Lassen Volcanic National Park in northern California to fight a forest fire. One of her co-workers is killed, but not by the terrible fire; a knife was stuck in his back during the firestorm.

Other exploits of Pigeon include a fire detail at an island in Georgia's Cumberland Island National Seashore when a local drug-enforcement plane crashes, and an adventure at Lechuguilla Cavern in New Mexico, where a friend is in a perilous situation.

In *Liberty Falling*, Molly has had by-pass surgery followed by serious complications. Pigeon takes a leave and flies from Mesa Verde to New York City to be at her sister's side. The subways of New York are a far cry from the copper mines of Isle Royale and other such places. Anna aches for the mountains, solitude and the smell of pine. She finds something akin on Ellis Island in the city's harbor. Moving in with a friend who had once been at Mesa Verde and who now lives on Liberty Island, she becomes well acquainted with the National Park Service boat schedule as she commutes between that island and Columbia-Presbyterian Hospital.

By now, the reader of the series is well acquainted with Anna Pigeon. Approaching middle age, she has served the Park Service for 14 years and is earning $36,000 a year. She supports vegetarianism; she has had experience with issues involving the environment and with domestic issues such as incest and child abuse; she is about to confront anti-authority paranoia and opportunity to use her E.M.S. training.

As Anna visits her sister, she becomes convinced that Stanton, her old flame, has fallen in love with Molly, despite the fact that she is considerably older than he. Anna is not really jealous; her chief concern is her sister's happiness. Stanton gradually persuades his ex-girlfriend friend that he is worthy of Molly.

While the psychiatrist's illness continues to run its course with ups and downs, there are two unexplained deaths on Ellis Island, as well as what appears to be an attempted murder when Anna herself is pushed into an on-coming subway train by a stranger (and then saved by another stranger).

By the end of the book, Pigeon has solved the mysteries, prevented the demolition of the Statue of Liberty, has seen her sister recover and made plans to return to Colorado.

*Liberty Falling* is contemporary, examples being references to Bill Gates, Prozak, Zoloft, DNA testing, mutant ninja turtles, and Beanie Babies. The descriptions of Ellis Island give the reader a sense of its former importance.

Barr's writings criticize various aspects of the National Park Service, among them low pay, low morale, red tape and tension between permanent and temporary workers. Larry Henderson, a veteran employee of the agency, notes that Barr is a fiction writer and is entitled to manipulate facts as she does.

Barr defends her criticism, contending that her aim is to entertain. Is that not a worthy goal of every mystery writer?

## *Listing of Works by Nevada Barr*

Nevada Barr does not use a pseudonym

### Anna Pigeon Series

*Track of the Cat* . . . . . . . . . . 1993
*A Superior Death* . . . . . . . . . . 1994
*Ill Wind* . . . . . . . . . . 1995
(published in England as *Mountain of Bones*)
*Firestorm* . . . . . . . . . . 1996
*Endangered Species* . . . . . . . . . . 1997
*Blind Descent* . . . . . . . . . . 1998
*Liberty Falling* . . . . . . . . . . 1999
*Deep South* . . . . . . . . . . 2000

### Historical Fiction

*Bittersweet* . . . . . . . . . . 1984

# 19
# Patricia Cornwell

Much of the writing of Patricia Cornwell (who is also sometimes known with the middle initial D.) focuses on the gruesome details of autopsies—not a subject likely to be popular with the public. Nevertheless, Cornwell's books are bestsellers that have emphasized the importance of the medical examiner in solving unexplained deaths. Perhaps this is to be expected—at age nine she wrote a poem about Lincoln's death, devoting a considerable proportion of it to his wounds. In common with Edna Buchanan, her sympathy is emphatically with the victim and his family.

She was born on June 9, 1956, in Miami to Sam and Marilyn (Zenner) Daniels. Her father was an attorney, having clerked for Chief Justice Hugo Black. Her mother had once been an airline stewardess. The parents separated when Patricia, sometimes known as Patsy, was five years old, she and her two brothers remaining with their mother.

Two years later, the family moved to Montreat, North Carolina. It was here that Patricia came into contact with the Bells, who had once been missionaries to China. Patricia has fond childhood memories of visiting Virginia Bell's kitchen, where often homemade custard sprinkled with nutmeg was to be found. Ruth Bell Graham, Virginia's daughter, was married to evangelist Billy Graham, and Patricia developed a strong affection for her. Marilyn Daniels, plagued by a mental illness, became unable to care for her children, and sought help. The Grahams placed the Daniels children with missionaries just returned from the Congo, while their mother was hospitalized. Patsy was not happy with the arrangement; she wanted to stay with Ruth Graham. Obviously, Patricia's childhood was difficult; she once told an interviewer that anyone who showed her the slightest kindness or warmth meant a great deal to her. She misssed her father and her paternal grandfather.

As a child, she dreamed of becoming a professional tennis player. When she realized that others would be better players than she, she gave up the idea. According to one web site, she has today great admiration for Billie Jean King. A good student, she also aspired to be an archaeologist. She entered King's College in Bristol, Tennessee. Then she, too, had a bout with mental illness and was hospitalized for anorexia nervosa and bulimia—she weighed 89 pounds. After recovery, she transferred to Davidson College in Davidson, North Carolina, from which she graduated with a B.A. in English. (She stated in an interview that *Uncle Tom's Cabin* was her favorite book.) Ruth Graham was influential in encouraging her to pursue a career in writing.

The year following her graduation, Patricia married Charles Cornwell, who had been one of her professors at Davidson. There was a 17-year difference in their ages.

Patricia, with an eye to becoming an author, found a job with the *Charlotte Observer.* At first she worked on the graveyard shift as a copy assistant for the newspaper's weekly television magazine. After letting it be known that she would prefer to be a reporter, she began to be assigned stories that "no one else wanted." Within six months, she was a reporter, and within 12 months, was covering crime stories. In 1980, the North Carolina Press Association gave her an award for investigative reporting that had produced a series on prostitution.

The next year, the Cornwells moved to Richmond, Virginia. Charles had decided to become a minister and study at Union Theological Seminary, where he and his wife lived in cramped seminary housing. Patricia was unhappy at giving up her newspaper job. By then she had discovered that she really wanted to solve crimes as well as write about them. However, she was able to keep her hand in at writing, although of a different type.

Cornwell, who is a Presbyterian, busied herself by writing a biography of Ruth Bell Graham. Published in 1983, it was praised by the Evangelical Christian Publishers Association. In an interview in 1992, Cornwell noted that Graham was one of the greatest influences on her life and like an adopted mother to her. (This despite a period of six years when Cornwell was not speaking to the Grahams; apparently there was disagreement over what should be included about persons other than Graham.) A second Graham biography by Cornwell was published in 1997, with the profits from it donated to the Ruth and Billy Graham Children's Health Center.

With one nonfiction book to her credit, Cornwell began to write what she intended to be novels. Often she used information she had gained while working at the *Observer,* and eventually she was creating crime fiction. Thinking that her plots should be more believable, she welcomed the suggestion of a friend that she should talk with Dr. Marcella Fierro, a medical examiner for the Commonwealth of Virginia.

As a result, Cornwell found that she knew little about many of the high-tech procedures used in forensic medicine. But the field fascinated her. In an effort to learn more, she often visited the medical examiner's office and interviewed staff members. In 1984, she was offered a paid position. For the next six years, she worked at the morgue, first as a technical writer and then as a computer analyst. She watched more than 100 post mortem examinations.

To have a slightly different perspective, she became a volunteer police officer, riding with the homicide detectives every weekend for three years. Her varied experiences in that area left her with a very high regard for the police. The Virginia State Lodge Fraternal Order of Police in turn honored her in 1999 with a Golden Shield.

Cornwell was not a fan of mystery stories. Her first attempts at producing crime stories were influenced by works of Agatha Christie, P.D. James, Dorothy Sayers and the like. After the rejection of three books, Cornwell tried to make her writing more realistic. She also decided that a minor character forensic pathologist whom she had named Kay Scarpetta would have a major role in the next book. The professional life of Scarpetta seems to have been inspired by the real-life Dr. Fierro.

The result of her effort was *Postmortem.* After it had been rejected by seven publishers, Scribner's accepted it, with an advance of $6,000. It won the John Creasey Award (British Crime Writers Association), an Edgar, an Anthony and a Macavity, the only novel ever to be awarded these four. Nine very popular Scarpetta books followed. On the other hand, Cornwell was concerned when she learned that a man accused of strangling had used means described in her writing.

In 1990, the year that *Postmortem* was published, the Cornwells were divorced.

Patricia Cornwell has recently written two books that feature Judy Hammer, a police chief, and a young male cop.

The blue-eyed, blond-haired author devotes herself to causes, among them literacy and forensic pathology, to both of which she has been exceedingly generous. Another of her interests is the promotion of blood donations.

She has visited Barbara and George Bush in Maine and considers them her friends.

In 1997, *Vanity Fair*'s Judy Bachrach wrote an article on Cornwell that included interviews with people who knew the subject. The portrait that emerged was not altogether complimentary. To illlustrate, Bachrach stated that Cornwell was briefly involved in a lesbian relationship with Mary Bennett, an FBI agent married to another FBI agent and mother of two children. Bachrach also pointed out that Cornwell had a fixation on Jodie Foster.

Fame and success have made changes in Cornwell's life. She maintains residences in Virginia and New York, also in London and the Caribbean. (As governor of Virginia, Douglas Wilder noted that his state was "the home of many esteemed writers, including Poe, Styron, Beattie, Cornwell.") She lives with many security precautions and sleeps with a handgun by her side. With little time for social life, she enjoys her wealth, flying in private planes and so on. She values privacy. When questioned about her sexuality, she once replied, "I don't believe people should be defined by their sexuality."

Cornwell's father died in 1996. Since throughout her early life, she had felt a sense of loss, she arranged contact with Daniels a few years earlier. Acording to Bachrach, fame and money have failed to bring Cornwell happiness. Around 1994, she was diagnosed as a manic depressive. With proper medication for the illness, her life has improved and become more normal.

Dr. Kay Scarpetta, the protagonist that brought Cornwell before the public eye, is the chief medical examiner of Virginia when she is introduced at age 40. Qualified in both medicine and law, she holds consultative positions as well—for instance, at the Federal Bureau of Investigation's Investigative Support Unit in Quantico. (*The Body Farm* by Cornwell is dedicated to Senator Orin Hatch, who was able to direct funds from the 1994 federal crime bill to the F.B.I. training academy.) Cornwell once noted that Scarpetta approaches cases with the physician's sensitivity, the scientist's rational thinking and a humane woman's concern for the sanctity of life. According to her inventor, Scarpetta is based on no particular person. The chief and deputy medical examiners have advised Corwnell about the accuracy of her writing, and both have influenced her portrayal of the character. *Body of Evidence* is dedicated to an FBI agent, Ed Sulzbach, from whom she learned much about profiling criminals.This technique is frequently referred to in the Scarpetta books.

A renegade Catholic, Scarpetta was brought up in a poor Italian neighborhood of Miami. Her father was sick for many years and died when she was 12. She is not particularly close to her mother, nor to her sister Dorothy, who writes children's books. Dorothy seems more interested in her literary career than in her daughter Lucy. Scarpetta married a classmate while in law school at Georgetown, but the couple parted after six years, both afraid of commitments. She becomes sexually involved with a few men and falls in love with FBI agent Wesley Benton. She describes herself as having "...the body and sensibilities of a woman with the power and drive of a man...." She knows her limitations, but demands respect when it is due. She once said in court: "...I am a medical doctor with a medical degree. I have a specialty in pathology and a subspecialty in forensic pathology.... Therefore, I would appreciate being addressed as Dr. Scarpetta instead of Mrs. Scarpetta."

Scarpetta is intent on solving murders, including serial killings. She uses the latest in technology, often working with experts in fields peripheral to forensic medicine. She is a woman of many abilities—for instance, an accomplished cook; she is able to scuba dive to inspect an underwater crime scene; and she takes tennis lessons. Her base is Richmond, but she gets around—for example, to London (by Concorde)—and she turns up at Interpol headquarters in Lyon when wanted there.

Police Officer Pete Marino is another important character in the Scarpetta series. He reflects Cornwell's sympathy for the police. Formerly a member of the New York Police Department, Marino has experience and common sense. Ignorant of the basic rules of English grammar, he is often crude and bigoted. More importantly, he has integrity and is dependable. Between Scarpetta and Marino exist mutual respect and affection. He even concedes that Scarpetta did not get where she is because she is a woman; she got there in spite of being a woman.

Lucy, Scarpetta's niece, is also part of the series. At the beginning, in 1990, she is 10 years old; four years later, she is 21. This is in distinction to her aunt, who ages in proportion to publication dates. To Lucy, Scarpetta is a combination mother figure/role model, in part making up for her mother's deficiencies. Presumably this role in some way satifies Scarpetta's maternal instincts. A graduate of the FBI academy, Lucy is a computer genius. But she has problems; she is a lesbian—and Scarpetta is very sympathetic to this; Lucy is also unstable and has habits that are self-destructive.

Stress sometimes overwhelms the medical examiner; for instance, in *Black Notice*, a power-hungry woman police chief plots to undermine her, to the extent that Scarpetta is impersonated on the internet and her password for email used by someone else. She has this to contend with while she grieves over the murder of her lover, Wesley Benton. To bolster her spirits at such times, she turns to her friend and psychiatrist, Dr. Anne Zenner. (Zenner is the maiden name of Cornwell's mother.)

The Scarpetta books are written in the first person, giving the reader a clear picture of the protagonist's thoughts. There are many references that make the reader aware that scenes are set in the late twentieth century. Among others are: Michael Bolton, virtual reality, computer virus, O.J. Simpson trial, Waco, caller ID, room key of plastic.

*Hornet's Nest*, a 1997 book by Cornwell, did not bring Scarpetta on stage. Apparently this was poor judgment, because the book was not as popular as the series books.

Are there likely to be new Scarpetta mysteries? Says Cornwell, "She is fascinating to me, and that is what I enjoy about writing the series: there is always something new that will try her talents and make her grow."

## *Listing of Works by Patricia [D.] Cornwell*

Patricia Cornwell does not use a pseudonym

---

### Dr. Kay Scarpetta Series

*Postmortem* . . . . . . . . . . 1990
*Body of Evidence* . . . . . . . . . . 1991
*All That Remains* . . . . . . . . . . 1992
*Cruel and Unusual* . . . . . . . . . . 1993
*The Body Farm* . . . . . . . . . . 1994
*From Potter's Field* . . . . . . . . . . 1995
*Cause of Death* . . . . . . . . . . 1996
*Unnatural Exposure* . . . . . . . . . . 1997
*Point of Origin* . . . . . . . . . . 1998
*Black Notice* . . . . . . . . . . 1999

### Judy Hammer, Virginia West, and Andy Brazil appear in

*Hornet's Nest* . . . . . . . . . . 1997
*Southern Cross* . . . . . . . . . . 1999

### Nonfiction

*A Time for Remembering: The Story of Ruth Bell Graham* . . . . . . . . . . 1983

### Novelette

*Scarpetta's Winter Table* . . . . . . . . . . 1998

### Juvenile

*Life's Little Fable* . . . . . . . . . . 1999

# 20
# Carol Higgins Clark

This author's books are distinguished by amusing characterization and situations as well as their unusual titles. Regan Reilly, her detective, is described as soft-boiled; Clark has said, "Because I use humor, it's hard to kill people."

Carol Higgins Clark was born around 1956 in New York. Her father, Warren Clark, was an airlines executive. His wife, Mary (Higgins) Clark, is today a top-selling suspense novelist.

Carol's childhood memories include telling stories (nothing boring allowed) around the dinner table—an asset that her mother claims is related to their Irish heritage. Carol also remembers that she loved Nancy Drew. And she enjoyed writing letters, a liking not held by many youths.

Warren Clark died before his five children were grown. His wife's first book was published in 1975, but she continued to work full time (at non-writing) to support her family. The second book required retyping, which was time-consuming before the days of word processing. Carol, home from Mount Holyoke College, volunteered to do it. She not only retyped the manuscript, but also made notes and comments—for example, she suggested changing some dialogue to make it more modern. She continued this practice with subsequent books by Mary Higgins Clark, no doubt simultaneously learning much about the craft of writing.

Incidentally, she once changed the names of bars in New York City, telling her mother that no one went to the places mentioned in the manuscript. Carol laughed when a review stated that the author (Mary Higgins Clark) "offers a well informed tour of New York's singles haunts."

After graduation from Mount Holyoke, Carol studied acting at the Beverly Hills Playhouse, living in Los Angeles for 10 years. Her credits include an appearance in *Secret Service*, a television series. She was the star in a "Good Morning, America" mini-mystery entitled *Who Killed Amy Lang?* In 1990, Clark appeared in *Uncommon Women and Others*, a play by Wendy Wasserstein, produced at Carnegie Hall in New York. She had the lead role in the film *A Cry in the Night*, based on her mother's 1992 book. The film was shown at the Cannes television festival, the Montreal Film Festival and nationally on television in the United States

Clark has used her theater training to record for Dove Audio several Mary Higgins Clark novels, as well as some of her own. Although her acting in time took second place to her writing, she believes that once an actor, always an actor, and hopes to return to the stage at some future date. She particularly enjoyed playing comedy and carried it into her books.

Clark's first book, *Decked,* was published in 1992 and introduced sleuth Regan Reilly. Since it dealt with a murder on a cruise ship, Clark was looking for a nautical term in the title. But she knew that *Cruising for a Bruising* would not do. Her mother suggested *Decked,* which became the first of four one-word titles, ending in"-ed," with a fifth promised.

She begins each project by researching the intended location—and she finds that going to Aspen, Colorado, for example, is no hardship. Although Aspen is currently known as a ski resort, she managed to weave into *Iced* some of Aspen's mining history. Likewise she read about tunnels built under big houses during Prohibition being used to store liquor—and incorporated this into the plot of *Twanged.* Background research for her stories takes much of her time, but she enjoys travel and acquiring new knowledge. Of course she also uses what is already familiar to her—for example, Oxford, England, where she had studied, is in *Decked.* She once dated a man who owned a pantyhose business, the type of business that plays a prominent part in *Snagged.*

Clark admits that there is some of her in Regan, whom she describes as single, 30 and having fun. She adds that something happens wherever Regan goes. However, the idea of having her mother a mystery writer came from the publisher, not the author.

The four published books have been best sellers. According to their author, they have been "great fun to do."

Clark's current home is New York. As 1999 ended, she was working on *Fleeced.* She and her mother, with whom she has a close relationship, enjoy discussing each other's work.

Regan Reilly is a P.I. based in Los Angeles, but she often leaves the area to carry on investigations. Her parents live in Summit, New Jersey, where her father has made a very comfortable living as a funeral

**Carol Higgins Clark by Herman Estevez. By courtesy of Lisl Cade.**

director; her mother is a successful author of mysteries. Regan is a college graduate and spent her junior year at Oxford University in England. Qualified as a lifeguard, she is five feet six, has dark hair, blue eyes, and white skin.

*Snagged* takes Regan to Miami Beach, where she becomes involved in the happenings at a pantyhose convention, where the life of the inventor of indestructible pantyhose is threatened.

The locale of *Iced* is Aspen, where Regan and her family intend to spend a Christmas skiing holiday. It turns out that she has little time to spend on the slopes. Valuable paintings have disappeared from the home of some jet setters. A likely suspect is Eben Bean, the genial caretaker who has confessed to 30 years of jewel thefts. Five years in prison and the luxury of living in a home (in the guest suite, no less) where the owners are seldom present have reformed Bean. But it takes Regan's intuitive trust in him and her detecting skills to absolve him, even saving him from murder. Bean also turns out to be the son of one of the personages in the story. The book is humorous and contemporary—for example, a computer business is sold for two hundred million dollars.

A glance at *Twanged* gives some understanding of Regan and how her creator keep the reader's interest, not only from the mystery standpoint, but by injecting humor. The book focuses on life in the Hamptons, a collection of beachside villages on the South Fork of Long Island.

Chaplain Wickham Tinka, 54, known as Chappy, is a millionaire, having inherited Tinka Tacks, a prosperous business, so far not seriously challenged by Post It Notes. Chappy's Compound was built on the foundation of his mother's old home. This huge edifice is obviously meant to resemble a castle, but looks more like something in an amusement park. (Every time one of the entrance doors opens, a few bars of "When the Saints Go Marching In" are heard.)

Chappy has a yearning to become an actor, despite advice from his teacher that the millionaire drop the improvisational acting class in which he was enrolled. And he has grandiose plans for his Compound. His idea is to build Chappy's Theatre by the Sea—one way to impress Hampton snobs with what an artistic and talented man he is. He dreams of presenting *Fiddler on the Roof* with himself in the lead.

Chappy has a particular fiddle in mind. It had belonged to 74-year old Malachy Sheerin, all-Ireland fiddle champion. He gave it to Irish-American Brigid O'Neill on her 25th birthday because of her promise as a singer and a fiddler. Legend had it that that there was a curse on the instrument should it leave Ireland—and this happens when Brigid brings it to the United States. The fiddle's added attraction for Chappy are the initials CT on it—Chappy's own initials. And what Chappy wants, he usually gets.

When he sees Brigid on television, he invites not only her but her band to play at the Melting Pot Music Festival on July 4 at Southampton. The invitation includes a week's stay at Chappy's guest house with all expenses paid. Chappy's intention is to steal the magic violin, exchanging it for a look-alike substitute.

Regan is called in to guard Brigid when the latter's family becomes concerned about her safety—she has been threatened and one burglary of the fiddle attempted. Regan is pleased to be hired because her mother and father are at the Hamptons, also Kit, her best friend, who sells insurance.

The cast of characters includes some real oddballs. One is an expert on feng shui, the Chinese art of placing special objects around the house so things go better—harmony and balance are the goals of his life. Another strange character is a man with an abnormal appetite for eggs. Peace Man, who refers to himself in the third person, shaves his head and is resident guru for Bettina. Bettina seems a bit strange, too. She is Chappy's wife, having remarried him recently when she found that his mother was dead. (She could not stand her mother-in-law, referring to her as an old bat.) A social climber, Bettina encourages Peace Man's strange ways.

There are several presumably minor characters, among them Darla Wells, an aspiring musician who is furious at Brigid because Darla's appearances on a program were cut in favor of the talented and popular singer from Ireland. Duke is Chappy's henchman, who botches the first burglary of the fiddle. Duke, as does his boss, has acting ambitions.

It is Regan's job to figure out who may be dangerous to her client. This she does, bringing the thwarted murderer to justice. Regan also saves Chappy from death. Grateful that his life has been saved, he is reconciled to the return of the violin to Ireland and agrees to fund the building of a music school in the West of the Emerald Isle.

*Twanged* portrays Regan at 31—still young enough that Carol Higgins Clark fans can count on many more adventures.

## *Listing of Works by Carol Higgins Clark*

Carol Higgins Clark does not use a pseudonym

*Decked* . . . . . . . . . . . . . . . . . . . . . . . . . . . . . . . . . . . . . . . . . . .1992
*Snagged* . . . . . . . . . . . . . . . . . . . . . . . . . . . . . . . . . . . . . . . . .1993
*Iced* . . . . . . . . . . . . . . . . . . . . . . . . . . . . . . . . . . . . . . . . . . . . .1995
*Twanged* . . . . . . . . . . . . . . . . . . . . . . . . . . . . . . . . . . . . . . . .1998

# 21
# Megan Mallory Rust

Megan Mallory Rust has served as an officer of the Alaska chapter of both Sisters in Crime and International Women Pilots. These memberships reflect two consuming interests of her life.

She was born on October 27, 1957, in an Air Force hospital in Mineola, New York, to Henry and Alberta Rust. She is "one quarter Scotch-Irish, mixed with English, German and Norwegian." While Megan was still a baby, her Air Force father was transferred to Anchorage, Alaska. When he retired as a lieutenant colonel, he started a flying service, later managed by his sons, Todd and Colin. This meant that Megan spent her childhood in Anchorage and that as she was growing up, she had a constant exposure to aviation.

As a youngster, she raised and trained a show horse; during her early teenage years, she competed in horse shows, winning a medal that entered her in the nationals held at Madison Square Garden. She also competed in interscholastic volleyball, basketball, and track. In 1974, she was a member of a girls' basketball team that won the Alaska State Championship. The following year, Megan graduated from West Anchorage High School.

She entered Washington State University in Pullman with the intention of studying biomedical engineering. After three semesters, she decided that this was not to her liking, and withdrew from the university.

Her father had never pushed aviation at her, but he did give her flying lessons as a graduation present—a present that she used after she had quit college. According to Megan, "I knew almost the minute I climbed into the pilot's seat that I wanted to be a professional aviator." She sensed that she was good at it. She also realized that being a woman in a male-dominated career field would be tough, and she planned accordingly. Her goal was to obtain a college degree in aviation, something that her male competitors might lack. By transferring her W.S.U. credits to Embry Riddle Aeronautical University in Daytona Beach, Florida, she was able to receive a B.S. in aeronautical science in 1979.

Her plan paid off; she soon found work as a flight instructor in an Army flying club, and part time in the same capacity at a civilian flight school. After six months as an instructor, she landed a good position as co-pilot on a DeHavilland Twin Otter, a 19-passenger twin-engine plane. When the company that employed her lost its contract with a regional airline, Megan quickly found work as co-pilot for a corporate aviation department on another large twin-engine plane known as Beechcraft King Air. But this was seasonal work and meant a lay-off in the fall.

Flying jobs for women were in short supply, and it was two years before Megan found another. This was with Hermes Air in Bethel, Alaska. On a June day in 1984, she had just returned from a flight to the village of St. Marys. As she walked across the tarmac, a forklift backed up and ran over her. She sustained a serious head injury and a crushed pelvis.

Megan lost consciousness and was flown to a hospital. A public health nurse aboard the plane resuscitated her twice when she stopped breathing. Slowly she came out of the coma, which lasted almost a month. From Anchorage she was transferred to Craig Hospital in Denver, a center that specializes in brain and spinal injuries. She spent five months there.

After a year of rehabilitation, when she re-learned how to walk and talk, she was functional by 1986; and she was convinced that she could fly again. However, residual physical problems deterred her from receiving medical certification by the Federal Aviation Administration.

Megan remembers that there was nothing for her to look forward to; "I figured I'd never find anything else that I'd enjoy so much." But she was wrong. She knew she had to do something productive: "I would not sit on my hands and profess being handicapped." After a couple of clerical jobs with Anchorage air carriers and a stint at computerized bookkeeping, she decided to pursue a bachelor's degree in journalism and public communication at the University of Alaska, Anchorage. Her idea was to use this training in an advertising career.

In an elective course in screen writing, an hour-long screenplay was an assignment. Megan wrote about a Bethel woman who flies. She recalls that the experience showed her how much fun writing could be. "Forget advertising," I told myself, "get busy building a career as a novelist."

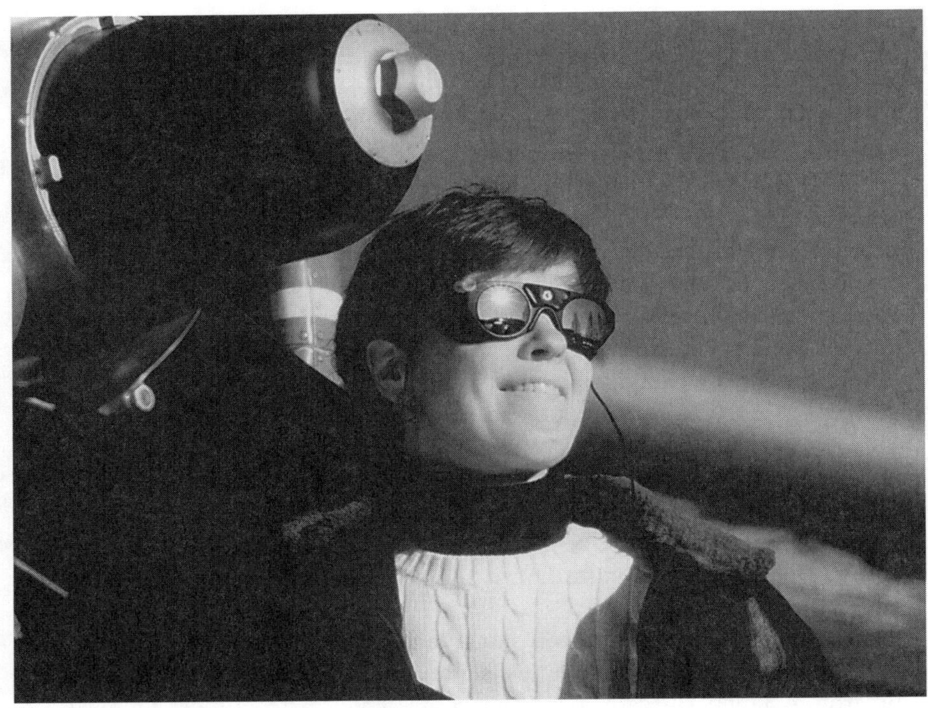

**Megan Rust by Third Eye Photography. In background is a Beechcraft King Air, the aircraft Morgan commands on the medical evacuations in the stories. By courtesy of Megan Rust.**

She was wise enough to write about a subject she knew well; her first manuscript was about a woman bush pilot in Alaska. It was rejected. She enjoys reading mysteries, so her next attempt was a mystery. It, too met with rejection the first time she sent it out. Convinced that the story had merit, she tried another publisher. When it reached Tom Colgan, a senior editor at Berkley Publishing, he was impressed; he considered it a good mystery with a great setting and really appealing characters. The upshot for the author was a contract for three books, with an option for a fourth. The protagonist/P.I. of the series is pilot Taylor Morgan, "She is my alter ego," explains Rust, "and through her I can continue my flying career." *Dead Stick* appeared in 1998. Holding a copy of that book in her hands for the first time gave her the same satisfaction that she had experienced on completing her first solo flight.

Additional Morgan Taylor books followed. Rust is also working on a second series with another heroine who is just as unusual as Morgan.

The author lives with her cats in Eagle River, Alaska, where she and William Berson, her partner for many years, built a home in 1995. Four years later, they added a natural rock patio. More landscaping is planned—she says there is always something else to be done.

Megan Rust is upbeat about her situation:

> Although my head injury has robbed me of many things (including my flying career), and has to be considered a tragedy, it probably was the best thing that ever happened to me. If my flying career had not been taken away from me, I never would have discovered writing. I never would have made much of a name for myself in aviation, though I'm hoping that I can do so with my writing.
>
> Plus, it's more fun.

It is obvious that this author does not lack gumption.

The P.I. in this series is Taylor Morgan. She begins as a confident, gutsy Alaskan bush pilot, then graduates to flying a sophisticated twin-engine Beechcraft King Air when she goes to work for Life Line Air Ambulance. She loves being involved in saving lives, especially when flying is part of it; according to her, flying is almost better than sex. Her language would horrify Miss Jane Marple—"fuck" seems to be the favorite word in her vocabulary. In contrast, she owns a Mickey Mouse watch. Most important, she has integrity and an innate sense of justice. Small in stature, she keeps fit by weightlifting. She has a boyfriend named Steve Derossett, who is also a pilot, and her former boyfriend, Jack Davidson, is a pilot, too.

*Red Line* (which marks maximum speed) develops the story of how Taylor solves attempted murder and, at the same time, shows how the greed of white men inflicted grievous harm on the Yup'ik people by smuggling alcohol to them.

The setting is southwest Alaska, in particular the region where Taylor flys a low-tech single-engine Cessna from village to village in the Yukon-Kuskokwin Delta. After three years of performing medevacs, Taylor is on vacation. But it is a busman's holiday—she is persuaded to return for a short time to Tundra Air Charter, her old stamping ground, to fill in for another pilot. This entails delivering groceries, soda pop, even disposable diapers; sometimes the cargo is human—she transports a Native boy wearing a Teenage Mutant Ninga Turtles T-shirt. It is understood that she is ready to accept medevacs should the occasion arise, although the Cessna is a far cry from the craft she is used to. The reader learns how primitive conditions are in some of the villages—for instance, some areas have no hangars; cargo is sometimes unloaded into wheelbarrows, and so on.

On the way to Goodness Bay with cargo, Taylor descends at Quinhagak because of bad weather. There she finds a health aide ready to transport a patient in critical condition to Bethel, but frantic because the medevac ordered from Bethel is delayed by the weather. Morgan takes them despite the deadly threat of icing, which her plane is ill-equipped to handle.

She learns that the patient has an illegal stash of liquor—illegal because he lives in a dry town. When he refused to sell to villagers who had already bought some, he was severely beaten in an attempt to make him tell where the liquor was stored. Then he was knived and left bleeding. Morgan is curious about who flew in the booze—for flying is the mode of transportation to that area.

The flight to Bethel is hair-raising. The flying conditions tax the ability of the pilot; she just misses collision with another plane. The ability of the health aide is taxed also: the patient stops breathing and requires recussitation. Nevertheless, he was delivered alive to the hospital. (Unfortunately he died a short while later.)

The only passenger on a flight from Marshall to Bethel is Kittie Avakana, a Yup'ik woman whom Taylor remembered from high school—their team had won the state basketball championship. Kittie, now the only nurse in Marshall, is flying to Anchorage to sell some beautiful baskets she had made. Taylor learns that Kittie's parents died in a snowmachine accident because they were drunk—drunk on liquor from a bootlegger. She begs her friend to find who is the bootlegger at Quinhagak.

Taylor has admiration and affection for the the Yup'iks and disdain for anyone who would encourage the use of alcohol in a town that had voted to be dry. The agent at Russian Mission had added to her concern by mentioning that he thought someone was smuggling booze there by plane. The aviatrix knows that her contacts with fliers would be helpful in an investigation, and she decides to accommodate Kittie.

The effort causes attempts on her life; at first, the state police fail to take her seriously. But she perseveres to see justice prevail.

There are descriptions of the Alaskan scenery, the effect of permafrost and the like. There is also evidence of a down-to-earth atmosphere—for example, when a landing in a remote place is imperative, Morgan by radio requests a ploughing of the airstrip, only to find that the driver forgot to put oil in the truck and it quit running the day before.

Rust says this about Taylor Morgan:

> Since her existence is so integral to the way I see myself, I hope to keep her going as long as I can. So far, I haven't run out of fresh ideas for her adventures, and I get a lot of enjoyment from writing about her.

## *Listing of Works by Megan Mallory Rust*

Megan Mallory Rust does not use a pseudonym

### Taylor Morgan Series

*Dead Stick* . . . . . . . . . . 1998
*Red Line* . . . . . . . . . . 1999
*Coffin Corner* . . . . . . . . . . 2000

### Completed but not published

*Graveyard Spiral*
*Bleed Down*

# Recapitulation and Afterthoughts

What do crime writers have in common? To examine this, we compare the lives and writings of the 21 authors featured in this book.

Their backgrounds vary considerably. Christie, Heilbrun, Sayers and probably Turnbull appear to have had carefree upbringings. On the other hand, Cornwell, Highsmith, and Rendell seem to have experienced stress during their youth. Buchanan and Pargeter came from families that lacked material goods; economic deprivation, however, was largely offset by their being loved. Presumably, the rest of the women lived in comfortable circumstances when they were growing up. The fathers of Allingham, Gallison, and Grafton were writers; the expression "ink in her blood" was applied to Allingham because several family members were professional writers. Barr found role models in some females in her family; Heilbrun followed advice from her mother, which meant essentially that Carolyn, the daughter, not emulate the mother, a woman who had no career outside the home.

During the 20th century, increasing and perhaps exaggerated importance was attached to attaining a college degree. Thus, it is not surprising that some of the older writers lack letters (for earned degrees) after their names. These writers include Allingham, Christie, Pargeter, and White. Although Pargeter had no degree, much of her life was spent in scholarly pursuit. A more recent author who did not graduate from college is Buchanan. Two women—MacKintosh and Rust—had postsecondary education in fields other than the humanities. Of the college graduates, Sayers was particularly proud of her Oxford education—something rather unusual for a woman of her day. Two women with advanced degrees and exceptional qualifications are Heilbrun and Paretsky.

The small sample used suggests that turmoil in an author's childhood does not destroy creativity, nor is lack of a college degree a deterrent.

It seems to this writer that all detective story authors are of necessity amateur psychologists if only because the chief investigator has to deduce something of the culprit's thinking. The works of Highsmith and Rendell in particular exemplify an interest in psychology.

Most writers read widely. Here are some of the literary influences referred to by the detective story writers under consideration. Allingham liked Stephenson; she also liked Shakespeare, and her favorite play was *Macbeth*. Buchanan, at age seven, relished Ellery Queen stories; *Raintree County* is a favorite with her. At an early age, Butler was impressed by *The Mystery of the Yellow Room*, and later by authors Queen and Daly. Christie's favorite book was *Bleak House*, while Cornwell's was *Uncle Tom's Cabin*. As a high school student, Gallison imitated Wodehouse. Grafton learned from her father and also from Leonard, Francis, Rendell, and Christie. As a youngster, Heilbrun liked the Nancy Drew and Judy Bolton books; later, she liked Woolf and Cather. Highsmith was drawn to Tolstoy and Dostoevsky. Mitchell liked Alcott, Compton-Burnett, Wodehouse, and Marsh. Pargeter was influenced by Kipling, Mallory, and Waddell. Rendell's favorite book is *The Way of All Flesh*; she admires *Crime and Punishment* and rereads *The Good Soldier*. White holds Austen, Waugh, Hardy, and Trollope in high regard. As would be expected, more than one is attracted to mysteries.

Economics plays an important role in most career decisions. Mystery writing was the first career of Allingham, Butler, Christie, and Turnbull. Most of the others had various means of support before attempting to live on their earnings as crime writers. Barr was an actress, and later worked for the National Park Service. Buchanan had valuable experience as a crime reporter. Clark was an actress (and is still interested in the profession). Cornwell was a journalist and computer analyst. Gallison held different positions over a long period. Grafton wrote screenplays and teleplays. Heilbrun was a university professor. MacKintosh was a physical training instructor. Mitchell was a teacher (and did not make a large amount of money from her writing). Pargeter was a pharmacist's assistant. Paretsky spent years in marketing. Rendell worked for a newspaper. Sayers was employed by an advertisement agency. Rust was an aircraft pilot. As noted by Gidez, White's best novels take place within the medical and administrative settings that she knows so well. The varied experiences gained by all are reflected in much of their writing, which lends good variety.

Butler believes that a mystery writer needs experience in living theater regardless of whether the writer has acting potential. Of the 21, Barr, Clark, and Marsh were professional actresses; Allingham began to train for a stage career but dropped out; White functioned as an assistant stage manager; Gallison was an amateur actress and puppeteer; Rust became interested in fiction writing while she was a student in a course on screen writing. Butler, Christie, Grafton, MacKintosh, Marsh, Mitchell, Sayers, and White all involved themselves in writing dramatizations. It would seem that theater experience is helpful to the crime writer.

As time passed, the appeal of writing mysteries took on a different form. Gidez observed that it was mainly Christie who, with *The Mysterious Affair at Styles* (1920), shaped the murder mystery into a standard form that remained popular for years—even if it tolerated what some critics have called wooden characters. She focused on the puzzle imposed by a murder, making entertaining reading with her expert storytelling. When White arrived on the scene, her focus was on the characters in the mysteries and their problems. This gave a writer to whom a social issue is/was important an opportunity to use the genre to publicize her message. This is apparent in the writings of, for example, Heilbrun and Paretsky. (In 1983, critic Clifton Fadiman wrote that Rendell and White "bring to popular crime fiction minds that are nourished and motivated by the social realities of Britain today.") To many, this new emphasis means that detective stories can also be straight novels.

It was implicit with the earlier writers that the guilty are punished. Highsmith took a different view in her Ripley series, producing entertaining reading. Gallison and Clark inject humor into their series, detracting from the usual seriousness of the crime novel, nevertheless holding the reader's attention.

Eleven authors saw fit to use pseudonyms. Their reasons vary, but all relate to the fact that the writer is trying to disassociate her name from what she has written. Pargeter had four pseudonyms, at least three male; Allingham and Mitchell had just one. MacKintosh used both male and female aliases. White used initials only, making gender identification impossible. Butler, Christie, Heilbrun, Highsmith, Rendell and Turnbull used female names—one only for each author. The infrequent use of pseudonyms later in the century may mean that the time had come when women mystery writers had gained sufficient self-confidence that they were not intimidated by critics.

Productivity is affected by when the author first achieves publication, that person's life span, and how long the author is actively working. The octogenarians Christie, Mitchell, Marsh, Paretsky, and Turnbull turned out many books. The output of Highsmith, dead at 74, was moderate, but still considerable. Allingham, who lived until she was 62, was very productive. MacKintosh wrote actively from 1929 until her death in 1952 at

55. Sayers was productive when she died in 1952 at 55; however, by then, her chief interest was no longer crime. The productivity of each author indicates talent, perseverance, and drive. During this century, life expectancy has been increasing. We assume that from the 12 living authors we can expect scores of new intriguing mysteries.

Does a successful career in crime fiction make for a happy home life? Allingham's husband, with writing ambitions himself, was in support of what she was doing. Butler has a daughter and was married for some 35 years before her spouse died. Although Christie's first husband left her, her second marriage was happy. Heilbrun has three children; she has celebrated her golden anniversary. Paretsky, mother of three, has been married for almost a quarter of a century. Sayers' husband was financially dependent on her; her son seems to have appreciated all that she did for him. Pargeter appears to have made for herself a career that did not include marriage.The sample shows that some of these women can have both successful careers and satisfying home lives.

Fictional characters are associated with their authors—Jane Eyre with Charlotte Brontë, Micawber with Dickens, Tom Sawyer with Mark Twain—and so on. In addition to presenting a plot that satisfies the reader, the crime writer must create satisfactory characters. When a character, usually an investigator, appears in a series, the writer is confronted with problems such as aging, providing a spouse and the like. Nevertheless, the depiction of this person is a way for the writer to get across his/her message if there is one, as well as ample opportunity to display storytelling skills.

Turnbull's Miss Silver appeared as a pleasant, dignified sleuth, who commanded and was worthy of the respect of the police. A spinster, she had taught for 20 years before becoming a detective. Armed with her faith in God, she depended on her knowledge of people to solve crimes. Her world consisted largely of people of independent means; but, for her, investigation was no hobby—she made a living at it. This idea was somewhat unusual, at least in the first half of the century. Possibly it was prompted by Turnbull's own experience at bread winning.

The Belgian Poirot was to Christie's reputation what Tom Sawyer was to Mark Twain's. Poirot was a professional—a retired police officer who became a private sleuth. Endowed with many talents, he was given to making unique pronouncements. In this, he was a contrast to the unimaginative Chief Inspector Japp, with whom he often worked. Poirot's investigations sometimes took him out of England, offering new and interesting settings. If British readers did not care for a foreigner, Captain Hastings was at Poirot's side, and if they wanted romance, Hastings sometimes fell in love.

Miss Marple was another enduring character of Christie. This sleuth had no professional training, gaining much of her knowledge of human nature from the people who lived in St. Mary Mead. Another elderly spinster, she was convinced that the wicked would be punished, and she often helped the police to find the guilty. In common with Turnbull, Christie used the investigators to entertain, rather than to educate or propagandize.

Sayers needed to make money from her writing, and she used the detective story to gain it. At the same time, she hoped to raise the level of the genre: Her Lord Peter Wimsey, an amateur detective and man of many talents, charmed her readers and demonstrated her literary skill.

Although MacKintosh depicted Inspector Grant in a favorable light, she emphasized the role of chief inspector to a lesser degree than had her predecessors. She even let him make some serious mistakes, which worked for good in that he became more sympathetic than the prototype investigator. Known as a "gentleman cop" because he was independently wealthy, Grant worked hard and was reliable and persistent. From time to time, there was a woman in his life, but it ultimately (in *The Singing Sands)* became clear that his devotion to work left no room for a wife. It is worth noting that one of his interests was actress Mart Hallard, whom MacKintosh portrayed as a single, independent woman.

Beatrice Adela Lestrange Bradley, the character created by Gladys Mitchell, first appeared on stage in 1929. Although not a detective by profession, she helped the police to solve many mysteries. A widow and the mother of adult children, she was qualified in medicine and held the office of consultant psychiatrist for the Home Office. She also had liberal ideas. On the whole, she was ahead of her times.

The exploits of Cambridge-educated detective Albert Campion were recounted by Allingham from 1929 to 1965. His adventures were concerned with with contemporary events and made interesting reading. Campion married a woman who became not only the mother of a son, but also an aircraft designer.

Pargeter wrote two mystery series—one set in the 20th century, the other in medieval times. The Felce family were the players in the first, with the father a traditional police officer. His wife was an opera singer, but Pargeter saw fit to have her give up her singing career when she married. The Cadfael series portrayed the author's skill in characterization and the use of historical materials in story construction.

Two series—one with a male and one with a female protagonist—are the products of White's imagination. The first is Dalgliesh of Scotland Yard, a well developed and attractive character. The second is Cordelia

Gray, young and less prominent in the criminal justice system, but on the scene in 1972 as a private detective. Besides inventing interesting characters, White is masterful in describing the settings, in which they react.

John Coffin and Charmian Daniels are Butler's professional police officers. Both are well developed, act in interesting settings and have contemporary problems to deal with. In contrast to Cordelia Gray, Daniels has had time to work up to a position of authority in which she is respected. Her husband dies and as she approaches middle age, she marries a second time.

Heilbrun created the first American female sleuth and named her Kate Fanslar. Fanslar, like Heilbrun, is a professor of English, associated with academic settings where literary quotes and allusions abound. She is Heilbrun's protagonist to show that unequal treatment of women in academe exists. The author holds interest by skillful plotting.

Inspector Wexford, invented by Rendell, is the last male police investigator in this book. Along with Alleyn, Grant, Dalgliech, Coffin and others, he is competent, hard working and respected. Like the Canadian Mountie, he is expected to get his man (or woman), and does. Dora, his wife, is not the self-sufficient woman that feminists admire, but nevertheless a modern housewife and as likable as her husband. The story lines of the series are interesting.

Buchanan's mouthpiece is Britt Montero, a Cuban-American crime reporter for the *Miami Daily News*. She is tough, thorough and devoted to her work—so devoted that she risks her life for the opportunity to interview a serial killer. Police Officer Kendall McDonald and she are attracted to each other, but he is no more likely than she to let career take second place to anything. Buchanan's knowledge and love of Miami are reflected in her reporter. (The latter suffers through both a hurricane and a drought; the drought is so vividly described that the reader almost feels the heat.) Montero has great sympathy for the family of a murder victim and is not prone to overlook unsolved crimes. In this, she mirrors Buchanan; in fact, the creation of a crime reporter stems from Buchanan's fervent belief that accurate reporting is an important aid to obtaining justice.

Nick Magaracz, private eye, and Mother Lavinia Grey, an Episcopalian minister, are contributed by Kate Gallison. The Magaracz series pokes fun at bureaucratic methods, but does little to project Nick as a brilliant investigator. The Gray books are amusing and simultaneously reveal in Mother Vinnie's concerns Gallison's social conscience. There is a contrast here between the thinking of Buchanan and that of Gallison: Gallison, through Mother Vinnie, supports gun control, while Buchanan does not.

Kinsey Millhone, dreamed up by Grafton, is a tough American private eye, with little resemblance to Miss Silver and her ilk. Inclined to be a loner, she has been divorced twice. She loves being single. And she does solve cases, some of them murders committed long ago. Grafton believes her role as an author is to entertain—just what Kinsey does so successfully.

V.I. Warshawski is another independent woman—a hard-boiled private eye, the creation of Paretsky. She also holds a law degree. Based in Chicago, she is involved in insurance fraud, arson, public corruption and such. Paretsky's background and social concerns display themselves in Warshawski's actions, making very good reading.

Critics have noted that Nevada Barr's decision to make her amateur sleuth a park ranger was a good one for several reasons, not least that Anna Pigeon would have a variety of built-in locations in which to function. The author's ability to describe nature, combined with her plotting ability, provide entertaining reading. An independent woman, Anna is a widow. Whether she will marry again is problematical.

Dr. Kay Scarpetta of Richmond, chief medical examiner for Virginia, sprang from the imagination of Patricia D. Cornwell. Although Scarpetta spends most of her time in the morgue, Cornwell keeps the reader interested with her characterizations and plots. Scarpetta has no biological children, but is substitute mother to a niece.

Carol Higgins Clark has a fictional private investigator named Regan Reilly. She is very different from, for example, Kinsey Millhone in that the author creates humorous settings. The Reilly books are witty, and Regan comes across as likable, if not so far, an outstanding detective.

Megan Mallory Rust's first book came out in 1998, so the development of Alaskan pilot Taylor Morgan is still in progress. Rust's treatment of the problem of smuggled liquor into Yup'ik settlements is a hint that Taylor may be a future champion of other issues. Rust's personal flying experience provides an authentic background for her plots.

The 20th century saw change in many aspects of life. The authors selected here give emphasis to the changes in the status of women. We should note that when the century began, aviation was unknown, thus depriving Taylor Morgan of her job; likewise for Anna Pigeon, because the National Park Service did not exist. Also, Mother Vinnie would have had a different title because the Episcopalian church did not ordain women.

Our first sleuths (and a sleuth was sometimes a sleuthess) had feminine names (Maud, Jane, and Beatrice), prefixed by Miss or Mrs. As time went by, the detectives had masculine or gender-neutral names (Britt,

Kinsey, V.I., and Regan). Shakespeare declared that a rose by any other name would smell as sweet, so perhaps the tendency to use men's names is insignificant.

For most of the century, fictional detectives were predominately men because the vast majority of real-life detectives were men, and their exploits made good reading. Miss Silver, Miss Marple, and Mrs. Bradley were drawn with enough skill and imagination to ensure their continuing popularity. Yet today, they would not serve as suitable role models. It is the fictional, self-reliant tough characters of the latter part of the century that are potential role models for modern young women. These characters represent careers in criminal justice, university teaching, law, theology, medicine journalism, and park management. The super woman is Scarpetta, who appears to be capable of taking on close to anything. Thus these invented sleuths might affect rather than reflect their time.

Women sleuths remain popular. According to Chaddock, in 1998 there were more than 600 detective series created by women, most with women sleuths sorting out the clues. The interest in mysteries on the part of the reading public is amazing, considering the statistics: in 1998, in the United States with a population of some 273 million, there were 18,890 deaths from homicides and legal interventions. (As a comparison, 63,813 persons died from diabetes mellitus.) Obviously the public has a fascination with murder and will demand more crime novels.

Critics now agree that the literary quality of mysteries should not be disparaged. *Books of the Century* included *The Mysterious Affair at Styles* because it ushered in the Golden Age of crime novels; G.K. Chesterton's words have proved prophetic:

> Not only is a detective story a perfectly legitimate form of art, but it has certain definite and real advantages as an agent of the public weal.

# Sources


Allen, Jodie T. "These Are the Good Old Days." *U.S. News and World Report*, Jan. 31, 2000, p. 36–38.

Bachrach, Judy. "Death Becomes Her." *Vanity Fair*, May, 1997, p. 146+.

Backerman, Jane S. "Interview with P.D. James." *The Armchair Detective*, Vol. 10, 1977, p. 55+.

_____, ed. *And Then There Were Nine … More Women of Mystery*. Bowling Green, OH: Bowling Green State University Popular Press, 1985.

Bargainner, Earl F., ed. *10 Women of Mystery*. Bowling Green, OH: Bowling Green State University Popular Press, 1981.

Bloom, Harold, ed. *Classic Mystery Writers*. New York and Philadelphia: Chelsea House, 1995.

_____, ed. *Modern Mystery Writers*. New York and Philadelphia: Chelsea House, 1995.

_____, ed. *Lesbian and Bisexual Fction Writers*. Philadelphia: Chelsea House, 1997.

Boken, Julia R. *Carolyn G. Heilbrun*. New York: Twayne, 1996.

Brabazon, James B. *Dorothy L. Sayers: A Biography*. New York: Charles Scribner's Sons, 1981.

Breunner, Borgna, ed. *The Time Almanac 2000*. Boston: Little, Brown & Co., 1999.

Buchanan, Edna. *The Corpse Had a Familiar Face: Covering Miami, America's Hottest Beat*. New York: Random House, 1987.

_____. *Never Let Them See You Cry: More from Miami, America's Hottest Beat*. New York: Random House, 1992.

Chaddock, Gail R. "Whodunit?" *Wellesley*, Winter 1998, p. 16–19.

Christie, Agatha. *An Autobiography*. New York: Ballantine Books, 1977.

Clark, Maureen. "Scene" [article on Megan Rust]. *The Mining Journal*, June 22, 1998, p. 7+.

Cooper-Clark, Diana. "Interview with Ruth Rendell." *The Armchair Detective*, Vol. 14, 1981, p. 108–117.

_____. "Patricia Highsmith—Interview." *The Armchair Detective*, Vol. 14, 1981, p. 313–20.

Cornwell, Patricia Daniels. *A Time for Remembering: The Ruth Bell Graham Story.* New York: Harper and Row, 1983.
Diefendorf, Elizabeth, ed. *The New York Public Library's Books of the Century.* New York: Oxford University Press, 1996.
Dubrin, Lyn. [article on Carol Higgins Clark]. *Distinction* (Long Island), Feb., March, 1998.
Dyer, Carolyn S., and Romalov, Nancy T., eds. *Rediscovering Nancy Drew.* Iowa City, IA: Iowa University Press, 1995.
*The Face of History. Time.* Magazine Covers, 1923–1990.
Feder, Sue. "Beloved Creator of 'Brother Cadfael.'" *The Armchair Detective,* Vol. 29, 1996, p. 35–6.
Gambino, Erica-Lynn. [article on Carol Higgins Clark]. *The Southampton Press,* July 23, 1998.
Gidez, Richard. *P.D. James.* Boston: Twayne, 1986.
Gruen, Bernard. *The Timetables of History,* new 3rd ed., rev. New York: Simon & Schuster, 1991.
Hagen, Ordean A. *Who Done It?: A Guide to Detective, Mystery, and Suspense Fiction.* New York: Bowker, 1969.
Heilbrun, Carolyn G. *The Last Gift of Time: Life Beyond Sixty.* New York: Dial Press, 1997.
_____. *Writing a Woman's Life.* New York: Ballantine Books, 1989.
Heising, Willetta A. *Detecting Women 2: A Reader's Guide and Checklist for Mystery Series Written by Women.* Dearborn, MI: Purple Moon Press, 1996.
Herbert, Rosemary. "All That Remains." *The Armchair Detective,* Vol. 25, 1992, p. 388–97.
Holder, Peter A. Interview with Clark 8/25/94 as reported on website.
Johnson, Paul. *A History of the American People.* New York: HarperCollins, 1997.
Keating, H.R.F., ed. *Agatha Christie: First Lady of Crime.* New York: Holt, Rinehart and Winston, 1977.
_____, ed. *Whodunit?: A Guide to Crime, Suspense and Spy Fiction* New York: Van Nostrand Reinhold, 1982.
Kelly, Katy. [Article on Carol Higgins Clark]. *USA Today,* March 19, 1998.
Kismaric, Carole, and Heiferman, Marvin. *The Mysterious Case of Nancy Drew and the Hardy Boys.* New York: Simon and Schuster, 1998.
Klein, Kathleen G., ed. *Best Known Mystery Writers: Classic to Contemporary.* Westport, CT: Greenwood Presss, 1994.
_____. *The Woman Detective: Gender & Genre,* 2nd ed. Urbana, IL: University of Illinois Press, 1995.
_____, ed. *Women Times Three: Writers, Detectives, Readers.* Bowling Green, OH: Bowling Green State University Press, 1995.
Kunitz, S.J., ed. *Twentieth Century Authors: A Biographical Dictionary of Modern Literature.* First Supp. New York: H.W. Wilson, 1955.
_____, and Haycraft, H., eds. *Twentieth Century Authors.* New York: H.W. Wilson, 1942.
Lewis, Margaret. *Edith Pargeter: Ellis Peters.* Mid Glamorgan, Wales: Poetry Wales Press, 1994.

Marsh, Ngaio. *Black Beech and Honeydew: An Autobiography*. Boston: Little, Brown, 1965, rev. 1981.

Mann, Jessica. *Deadlier Than the Male*. New York: Macmillan, 1981.

Martin, Richard. *Ink in Her Blood: The Life and Crime Fiction of Margery Allingham*. Ann Arbor, MI: UMI Research Press, 1988.

Mass, Jacqueline K.D. "On the Quest for Brother Cadfael." *The Armchair Detective*, vol 28, 1995, p. 424–28.

*The Mining Journal*. "Scene" [article on P.D.James]. Jan. 10, 2000, p. 7+.

*The Mississippi Writers Page*. "Nevada Barr," On web, updated Feb. 1999.

Nelson, Catherine M. "Trouble is Her Business." *The Armchair Detective*, Vol. 24, 1991, p. 260–70.

Pamak, Orhan. "A Taste for Death: Patricia Highsmith's Crime Time." *The Village Voice*, XXXVII, Nov. 17, 1992, p. 107–08.

Paul, Robert S. *Whatever Happened to Sherlock Holmes: Detective Fiction, Popular Theology, and Society*. Carbondale, IL: Southern Illinois University Press, 1991.

Pederson, J.P., ed. *St. James Guide to Crime and Mystery Writers*, 4th ed. Detroit: St. James Press, 1996.

Pike, B.A. "In Praise of Gladys Mitchell." *The Armchair Detective*. Vol. 9, 1976, p. 250–60.

Purcell, J.M. "The 'Amanda Cross' Case: Sociologizing the U.S. Academic Mystery." *The Armchair Detective*, Vol. 13, p. 36–40.

Rahn, B.J., ed. *Ngaio Marsh: The Woman and Her Work*. Metuchen, NJ: Scarecrow, 1995.

Ramsey, G.C. *Agatha Christie: Mistress of Mystery*. New York: Dodd, Mead, 1967.

Rancourt, Linda M. "Murder, She Writes." *National Parks*, Vol. 69, 1998, p. 30+.

Rendell, Ruth (photographs by Paul Bowden). *Ruth Rendell's Suffolk*. London: Hutchinson, 1992, (first published in 1989).

Reynolds, Barbara. *Dorothy L. Sayers: Her Life and Soul*. New York: St. Martin's Press, 1993.

_____, ed. *The Letters of Dorothy L. Sayers*, Vol. Two. New York: St. Martin's Press, 1998.

Rivière, François. *In the Footsteps of Agatha Christie*. North Pomfret, VT: Trafalgar Square Publishing, 1997 (originally published in France in 1995).

Robyns, Gwen. *The Mystery of Agatha Christie*. New York: Doubleday, 1978.

Rodell, Marie F. *Mystery Fiction: Theory and Technique*, rev. ed. New York: Hermitage House, 1952.

Roy, Sandra. *Josephine Tey*. Boston: Twayne, 1980.

Sanders, Dennis, and Len Lovallo. *The Agatha Christie Companion*. New York: Delacorte Press, 1984.

Sarjeant, W.A.S. "The Last of the Golden Age Writers: Gladys Mitchell 1901–1983." *The Armchair Detective*, Vol. 18, 1985, p. 351–60.

Sayers, Dorothy L., ed. *The Omnibus of Crime*. Garden City, NJ: Garden City Publishing Co., 1929.

Shaw, Marion, and Vanacher, Sabine. *Reflecting on Miss Marple*. New York: Routledge, 1919.

Siebenheller, Norma. *P.D. James*. New York: Frederick Ungar, 1981.

Swanson, Jean, and Dean Jones, eds. *By a Woman's Hand: A Guide to Mystery Fiction by Women*. New York: Berkley Publishing, 1996.

Taylor, Bruce. "G Is for (Sue) Grafton." *The Armchair Detective*, Vol. 22, 1989, p. 4–13.
Thorogood, Julia. *Margery Allingham: A Biography.* London: William Heinemann, 1993.
Tolkin, Bruce. "In Memory of Patricia Highsmith." *Los Angeles Times Book Review*, Feb. 12, 1995, 8.
Vasudevan, Aruna, and Lesley Henderson, eds. *Twentieth-Century Romance and Historical Writers.* Detroit: St. James Press, 1994.
Winn, Dilys, ed. *Murder Ink.* New York: Workman, 1977.
Wynne, Nancy B. "Patricia Wentworth Revisited." *The Armchair Detective*, Vol. 14, 1981, p. 90–2.

## *Contemporary Authors* (Detroit: Gale Research)

| | |
|---|---|
| Vol. 120 | Entry on Gallison |
| Vol. 129 | Entry on Paretsky |
| Vol. 132 | Entry on Buchanan |
| Vol. 152 | Entry on Clark |
| Vol. 161 | Entry on Barr |
| NRS Vol. 17 | Entry on James |
| NRS Vol. 32 | Entry on Rendell |
| NRS Vol. 41 | Entry on Pargeter |
| NRS Vol. 52 | Entry on Buchanan |
| NRS Vol. 53 | Entry on Carnwell |
| NRS Vol. 55 | Entry on Grafton |
| NRS Vol. 58 | Entry on Heilbrun |
| NRS Vol. 59 | Entry on Paretsky |
| | Entry on Marsh |
| NRS Vol. 62 | Entry on Highsmith |
| NRS Vol. 63 | Entry on Butleer |
| | Entry on Mitchell |
| On Line | Entry on Barr |
| On Line | Entry on Buchanan |
| On Line | Entry on Butler |
| On Line | Entry on Paretsky |
| On Line | Entry on Tey |

## *Contemporary Literary Criticism* (Detroit: Gale Research)

| | |
|---|---|
| Vol. 25 | Entry on Heilbrun |
| Vol. 46 | Entry on James |
| Vol. 48 | Entry on Rendell |
| Vol. 102 | Entry on Highsmith |

## *Dictionary of Literary Biography* (Detroit: Gale Research)

| | |
|---|---|
| Vol. 10 | Entry on Gordon Daviot |
| Vol. 77 | Entry on Wentworth |
| | Entry on Tey |
| | Entry on Mitchell |
| | Entry on Allingham |

## *Current Biography Yearbook* (Bronx, New York: H.W. Wilson)

| | |
|---|---|
| 1933 | Entry on Heilbrun |
| 1994 | Entry on Rendell |
| 1997 | Entry on Buchanan |
| 1997 | Entry on Cornwell |

### *Websites*

Cornwell, Paretsky, Rust

### *Information on web*

Barr, Clark, Cornwell

### *Personal communication*

Butler, Paretsky, Rust

# Index

*Italics denotes a photograph*